1995/1997

REEF NOTES

Revisited and Revised
by Julian Sprung

Book Design by Daniel N. Ramirez

Published by Ricordea Publishing
Coconut Grove, Florida 33133

First Printing July 1998

Published by Ricordea Publishing
4016 El Prado Blvd.
Coconut Grove, Florida, USA, 33133

To purchase back issues of *Freshwater And Marine Aquarium* magazine or copies of the original "Reef Notes" articles contact:
FAMA, 144 W. Sierra Madre Blvd., Sierra Madre, CA, 91024

Printed and bound by Arnoldo Mondadori, Verona, Italy.

Design and production by Daniel N. Ramirez
Cover photos by: Daniel N. Ramirez and Julian Sprung.
Fish: Red Hogfish, *Bodianus opercularis*, photographed at Coral World, Eilat, Israel.

ISBN 1-883693-21-7

Julian Sprung, 1966 - Reef Notes

This book is dedicated to Martin A. Moe, Jr., who amazed me when I was a very impressionable 12 year old seeing his vats and concrete raceways full of tank-raised marine angelfish.

Acknowledgments

The following people have contributed to this book either directly or indirectly through their work and exchange of ideas: Dr. Walter Adey, Marj Awai, Rick (Fish & Pet) Bell, Dr. Craig Bingman, Stanley Brown, Dr. Robert W. Buddemeier, Roger Bull, John and Patty Burleson, Dr. Bruce Carlson, Merrill Cohen, J. Charles Delbeek, Don Dewey and the Staff at FAMA, Dr. Phillip Dustan, Svein Fosså, Thomas A. Frakes, Bob Goemans, Santiago Guetierrez, Brian LaPointe, Karen Loveland, Dr. Frank Maturo, Scott W. Michael, Martin A. Moe, Jr. and Barbara Moe, Alf Jacob Nilsen, Dr. James Norris, Mike Paletta, Daniel and Carmen Ramirez, Terry Siegel, Bob Stark, John Tullock, Dr. John Veron, and Peter Wilkens.

Table of Contents

About the Author

Julian Sprung was born in 1966 in Miami Beach, Florida. He is a graduate of the University of Florida with a Bachelor of Science degree in zoology, and is an author, consultant on Aquarium design, and frequent lecturer on marine aquarium keeping. He has been keeping marine aquariums for over 20 years, and began studying marinelife along the shores of Biscayne Bay in Miami. Julian writes the monthly column, "Reef Notes" in *Freshwater and Marine Aquarium* magazine, on which this book is based. He has authored numerous articles in other publications such as *Seascope* and *Tropical Fish Hobbyist*, and was Science Editor for the quarterly journal, *Aquarium Frontiers* from 1993-1995. Julian also wrote and produced a video entitled *An Introduction to the Hobby of Reef Keeping*. In 1994 J. Charles Delbeek and Julian Sprung completed over four years of work with the publication of their book *The Reef Aquarium, Volume One*. They also collaborated on *The Reef Aquarium, Volume Two*, published in 1997.

Introduction

Regular readers of my "Reef Notes" column may remember that the period encompassed by this volume was marked by numerous gaps in its appearance in *FAMA* magazine. The sporadic appearance of my column was not a result of lack of material or any disatisfaction with the magazine. During this period I was simply busy with the day to day work at Two Little Fishies, travel, speaking engagements, completing *The Reef Aquarium* Volume One and Volume Two, and the other volumes of *Reef Notes Revisited and Revised.* As a result of the gaps in the appearance of my column, this fourth volume in the series encompases three instead of the usual two years.

The years 1995 through 1997 were marked by increased acceptance of natural systems for the creation of a reef aquarium. During this period I continued my research on aquariums established with Jaubert's plenum system. In my columns, included here, are the opinions I developed about this system and the proper ways to set one up and operate it. The columns also show the range of ideas other aquarists and I have had in exploring natural systems, biological filtration, the use of algae for filtration, and incorporation of refugium aquariums.

Control of pests such as the proliferating anemone *Aiptasia* is always on the mind of reef aquarists. Over the years in my columns I have covered many techniques for eradicating this pest, but this book contains a description of what I believe is the best means of controlling them, stinging them with the coral *Catalaphyllia jardinei.*

Another common problem that this book covers is the incidence of "RTN" (rapid tissue necrosis) and "bleaching" in corals. Coral diseases in aquaria are particularly common these days because of the increased popularity in the fast growing small-polyped stony corals.

Calcium additions, calcium reactors, trace elements, and alkalinity maintanence continue to be important topics. This

Note: **My revisions and other new comments will appear in the margin in bold type face. Original text from Reef Notes such as captions for diagrams will appear in plain (not bold) type.**

period in "reef aquarium history" saw the proliferation of designs for so-called kalkreactors, which use carbon dioxide to dissolve calcium carbonate. There is also an increased focus on the importance of trace elements such as iodine, often associated with success in the culture of corals.

The culture of the wonderful pulsing soft corals of the genus *Xenia* is a challenge that many reef aquarists take. In this book I cover the requirements of this fascinating soft coral.

There's also a column in which I describe the abuse by some USFW officers in the "enforcement" of CITES. After reading about this abuse of power, I hope that the reader gains an appreciation of the conflict involved, the need for education on the export side, the innocence of importers, and the need to re-examine the true purpose of CITES, which is a monitoring system.

And of course you'll find and possibly even enjoy some monster stories, miracles and my jokes that help keep the aquarium subject matter from becoming too dry.

As a supplement to the columns I've included an article about mangroves, which I wrote during this period. These trees are quite attractive additions to any aquarium, given the proper care.

Once again I want to thank FAMA editor Don Dewey for promoting the reef aquarium hobby and supporting my effort to keep aquarists well informed. It's hard to believe, but it has been nearly ten years since I started writing this column! I also want to thank Daniel Ramirez for putting this book series together with such a beautiful design, and for keeping it all on schedule.

Julian Sprung
Miami Beach, Florida USA
June 1998

January 1995

I apologize that my columns have been a bit sporadic lately, the reason has been the enormous amount of time required to finish *The Reef Aquarium*, a fantastic, information-packed and beautiful book that Charles Delbeek and I have been creating for the past four years...and now it's done at last. Well, I hope you all have bought a copy by the time this column appears! So much for blatant plugs. There is another reason I bring up the book now, and it has to do with my recent trip to Europe, made in part to observe the printing of the book, and in part to visit friends, eat well, see new places, and observe aquariums. I thought you might be interested in what I saw in the latter activity, particularly in Monaco.

After arriving in Zurich and spending a great couple of days with Peter Wilkens and his family, I headed off by train to the French Riviera. Whenever I mentioned the trip to Monaco, people always seemed to think the object of my interest there was gambling. No, I assured them, I was going to see a public aquarium primarily, and do a little sightseeing, time permitting. I know they were thinking, "Why would this poor fool travel so far to see an aquarium?" while I was thinking, "why would anybody travel so far to gamble?" Well, I arrived at the train station in Monaco early in the morning and was happy to learn that the Musee de Oceanographique was a mere 20 minute walk away. With my luggage in tow, the hike up the extended series of steps on the hill toward the museum was a challenge, especially in the unusually warm weather, and with little sleep the night before on the train.

Tom Frakes of Aquarium Systems helped me get in touch with Dr. Nadia Ounais from the aquarium and Dr. Jean Jaubert from the Centre Scientifique de Monaco. (This may seem confusing, but the Aquarium, Centre Scientifique, de Monaco, and Observatoire Oceanologique Europeen are separate but cooperating entities in the same museum building). Prior to my trip we had arranged to meet on this morning, and I would have a chance to see the aquarium and the research facility. I met Nadia and Pierre Gilles, and afterward Dr. John Chisholm and briefly, Dr. Jaubert. The following day I met with Dr. Jaubert and was able to talk with him at length. The Museum is built on a cliff overlooking the Meditteranean. The view is postcard perfect. Inside, the displays are wonderful. Those of you who came to MACNA V last last year saw the fantastic video taken at the aquarium that Tom Frakes was showing. The displays were breathtaking, full of fish and healthy growing corals, and there was some demonstration of the techniques used to affix propagated coral fragments to the aquarium walls with underwater epoxy.

Seeing the aquariums firsthand, what impressed me was that they were not just healthy, they were beautifully constructed and aquasacaped. All employed the simple system developed by Dr. Jaubert (see Frakes, 1993), but most of the public displays were partially open systems being fed new water from the Mediterranean. I saw one closed system display, and it was very nice too, though the water was noticeably yellower than the other tanks. There were numerous rare fish and especially healthy specimens of some common ones. I was entertained by an enormous, stunning yellow puffer fish that cruised by me, turned and winked its expressive black eyes as they bounced off the glass. It played a game with the triggerfish housed in the same tank. There was a piece of plastic pipe in the tank that they would take turns carrying by mouth, the other fish always attempting to steal the pipe. There were also freshwater displays and natural Meditteranean aquariums with live rock. Still, the Red Sea reef mesocosms were superb. And I suppose that is what you want to hear more about.

The aquascapes were dominated by several color varieties of *Stylophora pistillata*, plating *Montipora* spp., and *Hydnophora excesa*. There were two giant colonies of bubble coral, *Plerogyra sinuosa*, and numerous *Favia*, *Turbinaria*, *Pocillopora*, *Acropora*, *Fungia*, *Herpolitha*, *Galaxea*, *Pavona*, *Pectinia*, *Lobophyllia*, *Psammocora*, and *Seriatopora hystrix*. These were the dominant stony corals. Some smaller exhibits featured fluorescent *Catalaphyllia jardinei* and *Cynarina lacrymalis*. There were many other genera represented, though I didn't take notes. They probably have one of the largest captive coral collections. There were plenty of wonderful soft corals too, including *Xenia*, *Litophyton*, *Sinularia*, *Lobophytum*, *Sarcophyton*, and *Cladiella*. In the larger tanks the coral growth

Note: In my experience with the orange spotted filefish, *Oxymonoacanthus*, the availability of coral polyps to feed on does not guarantee that the fish will remain fat and healthy. These fish usually starve in captivity, despite the availability of the small polyped corals upon which they feed. They feed on the tentacles of *Acropora*, *Pocillopora*, *Seriatopora*, *Stylophora*, as well as other corals and even hydroids, *Millepora*, and zoanthids. The odd specimen will also feed on prepared foods, even flake food. Such specimens are very hardy and will live in captivity for many years, nibbling occasionally on coral tentacles, doing no harm, and feeding along with the other fish on whatever prepared foods are offered. These rare specimens that take prepared foods do so immediately. If an orange spotted filefish does not eat flakefood, it will not learn to do so later. It will starve.

appeared to be oozing over the substrate, thoroughly encrusting all surfaces. In some of the smaller exhibits one could see the propagated fragments taken from other exhibits and attached to the walls of the aquarium with underwater epoxy. Many of these new colonies had grown quite large. Some fragmented colonies could be seen hanging by monofilament line in the tanks... more about this later. The live rock was arranged in such a way that numerous caves were formed, and some of the tanks had large sections of rock that appeared to be suspended impossibly over the bottom. Back behind the caves in one deep tank, which began below ground level and extended taller than the viewer, was an illuminated blue background...normally something that looks fake, but in this case it was very effective.

In addition to the corals, close inspection of the rocks revealed some turf forming algae, coralline algae, sponges, vermetid snails, worms, and herbivorous snails. One tank had prolific growth of a kind of tiny brittle starfish. These were not just coral gardens. There was good diversity of life, much as on a real coral reef. The smaller displays were of course less diverse, but nonetheless quite healthy. A Red Sea parrotfish species was common in most of the large mesocosms as were Red Sea Regal Angelfish and numerous butterflyfish. One display had the Red Sea variety of the orange spotted filefish, fat and happy feeding on coral polyps. He had so much to browse on that no harm was done. The closed system tank had wonderful bushes of *Litophyton*, *Cladiella*, *Sinularia*, *Sarcophyton*, and *Lobophyllia*, and a *Chaetodon semilarvatus* in the same tank did not appear to be bothering the corals at all (don't try this at home folks).

I talked to Dr. Jaubert about the American interest in his technique that has arisen as a result of Tom Frakes' article and showing of the video. We also discussed protein skimming calcium and trace element additions, and the purpose of the plate and isolated body of water below it. I was happy to discover that Dr. Jaubert (and everyone else I met there) was quite open to discussing his systems and receptive to possible modifications and/or additions. It was obvious that these simple systems were working quite well, but what advantages might be had by incorporating, for example, protein skimming, trace element addition, and kalkwasser? As Dr. Jaubert is currently researching calcification and coral growth, he is most interested in techniques that might affect calcification and growth.

He told me that he planned to make comparisons of his systems run with and without protein skimming. I asked him a question that some aquarists have asked me... "if the denitrification in the bottom substrate depends on organic material as food, would protein skimming be detrimental because it removes dissolved organic compounds that might be the bacteria's food?" Immediately Dr. Jaubert laughed and said no, there's plenty of particulate organic material in the substrate to keep the bacteria fed. I agreed, but added that it would be interesting to compare the functioning of the bed in aquariums with and without protein skimming to see if there might be any differences. So I look forward to hearing what Dr. Jaubert finds out.*

*In my experience protein skimming does not prevent denitrification, but I have not tested whether it can significantly limit the capacity of the bacteria to denitrify. I have systems employing Jaubert's method run with and without protein skimming, and all have a nitrate level below the detectable range of low-range hobby test kits.

Regarding calcium, if you recall, Dr. Jaubert relies on dissolution of the calcareous gravel to supply it. He claims the ability to maintain above saturation levels by this simple process of dissolution of gravel. I have seen this to be true in aquariums that retain CO_2. The lowered pH causes the gravel to dissolve sufficiently to keep the water very hard. I asked him whether he filtered the tap water before using it to replenish evaporation, and he said that he always used the water right from the tap, without any filtration. I pointed out that this was certainly a source of trace elements, and probably some calcium. He said that there was some calcium in the water. I tested it, and found 75 ppm calcium using Aquarium Systems' new calcium test kit. That's pretty hard!

**This does not work in aquaria heavily stocked with growing small polyped stony corals and live rock coated with coralline algae. Jaubert's systems have very little

I believe it is possible to use Jaubert's method to keep alkalinity and calcium high**, but what about the other benefit of kalkwasser?, namely precipitation of phosphate. Without protein skimming to remove some phosphate, it must be bound with organic detritus and with the calcareous gravel in Jaubert's system. Since the heterotrophic denitrifying bacteria consume detritus it is safe to presume that some Phosphate ends up in their living tissues, but what

ock in them and much
iore exposed surface
f aragonite gravel
han typical American
eef Aquariums.
aubert has observed
hat at some point the
rowth of corals may
xceed the rate of cal-
ium and alkalinity
eplenishment from the
issolution of the grav-
l. In his lecture at
IACNA he pointed out
hat in aquariums with
igh rates of calcifica-
ion the dissolution of
he gravel is not suffi-
ient to sustain the
rowth, hence the
ddition of kalkwasser
r other means of cal-
ium replenishment are
equired.

about the phosphate precipitated on the calcareous gravel? When the gravel dissolves, some phosphate must be liberated. This phosphate presumably binds to other gravel or organic detritus in the gravel bed before it can enter the water column. So the net result should be a phosphate rich bottom, which is not different from nature. Dr. Jaubert agreed, but added that this does not matter since the precipitated phosphate is not readily soluble. Still, I wonder how the accumulation of phosphate in his systems compares to ones using protein skimmers. Peter Wilkens believes that the primary benefit of daily kalkwasser addition is the precipitation of phosphate from the water, allowing the best environment for the corals to grow. I wonder whether the supersaturated calcium levels and alkalinity in Dr. Jaubert's systems doesn't also result in low dissolved phosphate.

I saw the labs where they were propagating *Stylophora, Galaxea, Favia,* and *Psammocora* primarily, and some *Porites, Acropora, Turbinaria,* and others secondarily. The colonies were being cloned by simple fragmentation. Some colonies were suspended in the water by monofilament line in order to grow them into spherical shapes with tissue ideally covering the entire surface so that no algae can attach. Other colonies were maintained on screened trays, and these specimens had to be disturbed periodically to keep them from attaching. Still other colonies were growing onto cut PVC pipe or sheets. These clones were being used in experiments with different nutrient loads or other water quality parameters to observe the effect on metabolism, health and growth. It was necessary to prevent algae growth on the clones not only for their health but also for accurate measurement of oxygen production rates (a measure of metabolism) during experiments in small respirometer chambers.

To observe the junction between tissue and skeleton, Dr. Jaubert grew colonies on glass slides, affording a uniform surface that light can pass through. With these colonies one could use a scanning electron microscope to photograph in perfect detail the structures at this junction between skeleton and tissue. He was using radioactive labeled calcium to trace the path of its deposition. Only bare calcium ions were small enough to pass through the calcium channels, and the deposition rates he observed do not agree with the well accepted, light-enhanced calcification hypothesis. The work being done at the Observatoire Oceanologique Europeen is being funded by the French government, and this in combination with the thriving coral mesocosms in the public aquarium located in the same building and limitless supply of good seawater has afforded rare opportunities to make significant contributions to the understanding of calcification, coral metabolism, and reef ecology. The working space in the labs with state of the art equipment and a breathtaking view of the Mediterranean is like nothing I've ever seen at any university. When I was there, several visiting coral reef biologists were using the facility to do research. The work is being published in scientific journals and, hopefully there will be time for articles for the aquarium hobby. The next issue of *SeaScope* from Aquarium Systems, Inc., which will be distributed before this column appears, will feature an update by Tom Frakes on the work being done in Monaco.

Algae monster visited AGAIN???
I have to tell you folks, I get a lot of letters. Generally they fall into a few categories: "I bought all this equipment so what do you think? and by the way I have this nagging problem with algae..."; "I can't seem to keep fish alive...and I have this algae problem too..."; and, "O.K., so I've read all of your suggestions about how to prevent and control algae, but what should I do to control MY SPECIAL CASE problem algae?" Judging by the letters it appears algae is the number one problem. I have covered the subject many times, and the algae have not since evolved to have different requirements. Here is a perfect sample letter that covers many bases. Considering the numbers of new reef aquarists who begin reading reef notes each year without benefit of seeing past issues of FAMA, it might be a good idea to have an annual algae column and, though much of the info will have been said before, perhaps some additional suggestions will be made...for example, see the remarks about hermit crabs to follow.

Q. Dear Mr. Sprung: I have been a salt water enthusiast for about 15 years now. About 2 years ago, I finally got with it and set up a reef tank. Subsequently, I received a visit from the algae bug (no surprise, right?). But this was no ordinary algae bug. Quite frankly, Mr. Sprung, I have done everything short of Clorox-ing the tank to get rid of this problem.

My first suspicion was, of course, that my phosphates and/or nitrates were too high. This I discerned due to the extensive reading I was doing on the subject, and that's what all the experts said was the most common cause. However, the tank tested zero for phosphates and very low for nitrates (around 2 ppm on a LaMotte test kit). I have also tested the make-up water, salt, carbon, etc. All are nitrate and phosphate free.

My next thought was that the temperature in the tank was too high. Living in Texas, it's hard to keep a tank at a decent temperature, so I purchased a 1/4 hp Aquanetics chiller, which easily keeps the 55 gallon tank at 76 degrees. No results. The algae just kept on growing. Next I turned to my lighting. I tried just about every type of bulb and combination thereof. No difference. The algae would grow even in low light conditions, although not as quickly. Next I switched from a homemade skimmer to an Emperor Aquatics venturi skimmer which I believe will handle up to 220 gallons. Nothing.

Ozone. I'd heard it was the cure-all for excess nutrients in an aquarium. So I purchased a 100 mg/hr Sanders ozonizer and Sandpoint controller. Cranked that old redox up to 390 mV. No algae in its right mind could withstand such an onslaught, I'd read. Wrong. Never even slowed it down.

At this point, I thought I had figured it out. I called John Tullock and explained my situation. He confirmed my suspicions by stating that my live rock was to blame. I needed to start over. So, after trashing my existing rock (Florida live rock, about 100 lbs. of it), I swallowed this bitter pill and ordered cured live rock from Reef Displays of the Florida Keys. Of course, I would have ordered from John, but I just simply could not afford the $6 a pound he sells it for.

I cleaned my tank very thoroughly, yanked the bio-balls from my wet/dry (to give the old Berlin method a try), and proceeded to build my reef. After about a month, guess who came back to visit? Yep, it started right where it left off. The tank has been set up now for about 3 months, and it is all I can do to keep ahead of this accursed algae. Seriously, Mr. Sprung, I have thought about quitting the hobby altogether. I can only take so much.

I can't understand, though, why others do not have this problem. Others with half the equipment and who spend a tenth the amount of time I do on mine. I have never even seen this type of algae in anyone else's reef tank. My algae is a dense green-mat type of algae that covers every exposed area of the live rock. It does not grow where there is no light, i.e. on the backs of the rocks. Scrubbing the rock only makes it come back more ferociously. The rock has a lot of calcareous algae on it, and the mat will usually grow right over the calcareous algae. I have lost a lot of specimens to the algae, especially open brain corals, which are overtaken rather quickly.

I run my tank at 1.024 S.G., 420 ppm calcium, 12 dKH. I use X-nitrate, X-phosphate, Superchem, Sandpoint carbon, Purigen, and Poly Filters. my additives include Kent Superbuffer and Iodine Supplement, Liquid Gold, and Seachem Reef Calcium.

Please, Mr. Sprung, if you have any recommendations regarding this problem or if you have ever seen this condition before, I would appreciate hearing from you. Sorry this letter is so long, but it's been stewing for two years.

Thank You for your time, Mike Osgood, Baytown, TX

A. Leave it to a Texan to have the world's biggest algae problem. I had to type your letter in the column in stages because your misery was hard to take all at once.

You said "the tank tested zero for phosphates", and that the "experts" claimed excess phosphate was a common cause of algae blooms. This is a common observation by exasperated, algae obsessed aquarists, and although I have tried (through repetition) in this column to explain that phosphate is seldom measurable in the aquarium water, the message falls on deaf ears most of the time. How can it be that phosphate causes the problem and the water test shows no phosphate? Simple, the phosphate is in detritus on the bottom and in the rocks, and it is bound with organic compounds which do not allow it to be measured by a simple INORGANIC phosphate test kit. This is not news for most readers of this column who are probably skipping ahead right now. The problem is that since phosphate test kits are popular items, and since phosphate is known to stimulate algae, the new aquarist must (necessarily?) be initiated in our hobby by becoming totally confused by the contradiction of algae growth and no measurable phosphate. This is a shame because the result is a lot of people giving up and quitting the hobby.

Phosphate test kits are best for testing tap water or activated carbon as potential sources of phosphate. Tap water in many areas does have measurable quantities of inorganic phosphate, and some activated carbons leach phosphate, so they can be a source. You indicated that you have tested the tap water but, surprise, it can have organic phosphate in it too, and that would not show on the test. Furthermore, it is natural to be adding phosphate to the tank with the food. One cannot prevent it, and small phosphate inputs are essential to the health of the system. To make you feel more exasperated, Mike, I should add that even when phosphate sources are restricted and the level of total phosphate is low, algae can make use of what little inputs there are and still bloom. This information has been covered in this column and of course it is explained in the new book.

Ok, so you want to know how to get rid of the stuff now, right? I have a solution for you Michael. My company has developed a device that has a key pad and blinking lights and a digital readout. There are two models, the one with four lights is more expensive than the one with three. We have found that the extra light is more effective at hypnotizing the algae, a new approach. This only works if you add the developer plant destroyer solution to the aquarium every other day and TELL the hypnotized algae it is getting sleepy, dying, going away, fading into nothing. In the meantime the digital readout affords a measure of how much time and money you've been spending. Well, the point of my exercise in sarcasm is to make you more aware of the need you express for a magic cure. Each time you have made a change (and purchase) for your tank you secretly told yourself that THIS was the answer, the secret magic solution to the problem algae. You have, as you call them, "suspicions". Well, I don't want you to ever give up the valuable disposition of hope and optimism, but the search for the holy algae grail should be discontinued. Manufacturers of such things as baldness cures, wrinkle removing creams, and other items know about human nature and the need for magic potions, and they make products you think you need that don't work. You can get the algae under control, but not with this magic-solution seeking approach.

As you've read before, for sure, algae control involves nutrient input and export management and the use of a variety of herbivores. Both are required for consistent results. Control of inputs involves filtering make-up water, limiting feeding, and avoiding the types of activated carbons that leach phosphate. Exports are achieved via protein skimming, detritus removal (which involves water flow, settling and removal, and detritivores), and algae filtration if employed. Herbivores I will cover in a moment.

The use of reverse osmosis and or deionization to treat the make-up water helps limit algae- stimulating nutrients. Be aware of the important point made by Albert Thiel at the Southwest Marine Aquarium Conference this past Spring regarding reverse osmosis or deionization. If the source water has a very high level of phosphate, nitrate or other pollutants, and the R.O. or deionizer alone remove approximately 95%, the remaining 5% can be significant. This is not a flaw in either method, but the point is that some areas have water so loaded with nutrients that one must prefilter the water before the R.O. and post filter it with a deionizer to remove most of the remaining 5%. In most areas this combined set up is NOT required, R.O. or deionization alone being quite sufficient, but in some areas the water is really bad. Some places have such good tap or well water that no filtration is required at all.

Protein skimming is your number one aid to exporting nitrogenous compounds and phosphate. It is not enough to have a protein skimmer with good contact time, it must process the tank volume frequently enough to be effective, and it must have sufficiently dense bubble production to collect the pollutants effectively. Good water circulation helps prevent nutrient rich detritus from settling in the rocks and bottom, suspending it so that filter feeders can eat it or so that it settles in the sump from where it can be siphoned off. Increasing circulation via powerheads and wave timers often dramatically curtails algae growth, a point made by Michael Paletta in a recent article in Aquarium Fish Magazine, though the Texas variety of hair algae sounds like it would just string out into the current and form waving bushes (that was supposed to make Mr. Osgood laugh).

Herbivores need to be varied and in sufficient quantity. In a 55 gallon tank I would recommend either a sailfin tang or a yellow tang, about 30 to 50 *Astraea tectum* snails, two or three *Turbo* snails, and 20 or more tiny hermit crabs. Tiny hermit crabs? Maybe you haven't had a chance to see Alf Nilsen's or Greg Schiemer's articles in "Aquarium Frontiers" journal, detailing the use of tiny hermit crabs for control of algae. There are a variety of species that remain small (less than one inch) and don't bother corals. Furthermore they are good algae grazers. Uh-oh, you did it again. The magic solution...I know that's what you were thinking. No, hermit crabs alone aren't the answer, but they do play an important role in helping to control the algae, as do the other herbivores. Don't forget to supply extra quantities of small shells for them as they grow.

The suggestion by John Tullock might have helped. Consider as well that dense heavy rock at $2/lb is not cheaper than lightweight rock at $6/lb. The volume the rock fills is more important than the weight, and the more expensive rock may fill volume with less weight, making it really equivalent in price to less expensive rock. There is a subtle effect of microorganisms and live rock that does affect the propensity to algae free or algae plagued tanks, and this is something that will take more research to elaborate...something for a future column about problem algae.

Since you asked me, if I had charge of your tank I'd make the following changes, not intended to discredit the value of the products you are using that many aquarists use successfully, but to change it to the kind of more natural system that I maintain, that has afforded good results for me. The purchase of a chiller was wise. Keep using it. The removal of media was also good. I don't use or recommend phosphate and nitrate removing media, so I'd take these out too, leaving just activated carbon in the system. I use calcium hydroxide in the make-up water, and find no need to add other forms of calcium or buffer.* Please see the previous Reef Notes column about calcium. Regarding trace elements, there are numerous products available that work well, including one that I sell. All I can say is you should add trace elements as a part of long-term maintenance, but beware that they are not magic either. Also, trace elements typically will make a problem tank worse and a good tank better. They make things grow. If your tank has desirable growth it will grow more. If it has undesirable growth, that will grow more. Until you solve your algae battle you should limit the trace element inputs or stop altogether. One piece of technical gadgetry that is helpful is a pH meter. Sell the ozonizer and redox equipment and buy a good pH meter if you don't already have one. By using kalkwasser and a dosing system (level switch and pump) you should be able to elevate the pH of the aquarium during the day to 8.4 or a little higher, but not over 8.5. This does reduce algae growth and stimulates coralline growth. Continue using the protein skimmer with air only. Finally, increase circulation, add some of the creatures I mentioned, and some coral sand on the bottom (about an inch) for denitrification. The nitrate you have is significant enough to stimulate algae growth, and reducing it would help you control the algae.

The live rock is probably ok if it still has good coralline algae covering it. It would take too much space to cover all the aspects I have touched upon here. You have some more reading to do.

Something to think about...
Several months ago I bought a magnificent book that you all should own, called *Aquariums: Windows to Nature*. It

*In some aquariums the rate of evaporation is so low that kalkwasser alone, added as top-off water, will not sufficiently keep up with the depletion of calcium and alkalinity. For these aquariums it is possible to add a strong, stirred, milky solution of kalkwasser dropwise at night via a dosing pump, or to use one of the balanced-ion calcium buffer solutions now available. The addition of kalkwasser at night takes advantage of the availability of respired CO_2 in the water. The kalkwasser added at night elevates the pH when it would otherwise fall. Thus it tends to stabilize the pH and promote higher alkalinity.

surveys the history of aquariums and describes unique exhibits and research done at public aquariums around the world. It is full of interesting information and breathtaking photographs. Among many insightful comments, one passage in particular caught my attention

"Natural exhibits usually exclude human beings or mention us only as intruders, bunglers, or fixers. Our species and our cultures have been deeply influenced by the waters on which we have lived, from the Pacific islands to African lakeshores to the edges of melting glaciers. The aquariums of the next generation will be more comprehensive in their interpretation of living systems and ecological dynamics." -- Leighton Taylor

This is a refreshing perspective. It seems to be a commonplace implication in the national news media, "environmental" movement literature, and even aquarium publications that the earth is a static system and man-made changes are irreparable and not a natural part of the environmental changes that happen whether we like them, cause them, or not.

Literature cited
Frakes, Thomas. 1993. Red Sea Reef "Mesocosms" in Monaco. *SeaScope*. Fall 1993.
Taylor, Leighton. 1993. *Aquariums: Windows to Nature*. Prentice Hall, New York, NY 190 pp.

March 1995

Q. Mr. Sprung, I have been keeping a large reef aquarium for approximately five years. My aquarium is stocked with soft corals and disc anemones, although I also have a significant number of hard corals (different species of brain, elegance, plate). The soft corals and disc anemones are growing extremely well, as are most of the hard corals (although I have lost the ability to keep hammer coral alive in this tank). Recently I was able to purchase a few small colonies of *Acropora* which I had every confidence would thrive in my system. Alas, they bleached and died within one month. My question to you is why? I have constructed my aquarium to be very similar to the system described by Alf Nilsen (excepting an algae scrubber patterned after *Dynamic Aquaria* by Adey, which after 3 years of operation seems to want to grow only pink/purple coralline algae). I routinely add calcium hydroxide and strontium chloride made myself, as well as CombiSan. The lighting is an Osram 250 watt powerstar. I have plenty of circulation in the tank. I am lost for an answer as to why I could not keep *Acropora*. Should I try adding CO_2 ? (I have an automated system in the closet that is unused). Ozone? Are all my soft corals leaching a substance into the water that makes *Acropora* unhappy? Is my lighting too bright? Could the fact that my tank is epoxy coated plywood be affecting the hard corals? If you have any suggestions I would welcome them.

Simon D. Ellis, Mahwah, NJ

A. With the greater availability of *Acropora* species lately in North America this question has been growing in popularity. When an aquarist asks me why a certain specimen died, I sometimes reply, "because it lived." Usually this attempt at bringing humor to the moment goes over poorly, and I have to go through a series of explanations and questions to cover the range of common causes of death in the particular species of coral, fish or whatever.

There are are over 100 described species of *Acropora*, and numerous varieties of each species. One must understand that these different species and varieties vary in their requirements and hardiness. Some *Acropora* are extremely hardy and adapt well to captivity, growing so strongly that they must be pruned regularly to prevent them from over-shading everything in the tank. Other species do not do so well in captivity, at least newly imported whole colonies of some species don't do well. Often, difficult species can be grown if one starts with a fragment instead of a whole colony. It seems that fragments adapt to new conditions (light intensity and spectrum, water quality) more readily. Once established and attached to the rock, a fragment can grow into a nice sized colony in less than one year.

One of the most critical factors in successfully growing *Acropora* species is maintenance of the water quality via the addition of trace elements, the minor element strontium, and calcium hydroxide. Your routine sounds fine, so we can assume that a deficiency was not the cause of your failure.

Another important requirement for some but not all *Acropora* species is strong water movement. It sounds like you have that one pretty well covered too. By the way, *Euphyllia* species do not like excessively strong water motion, and this may be a factor in your lack of success with hammer coral. One thing you did not make clear...did you lose a hammer coral while the *Acropora* was alive? If so, see my comments about protozoan infection below. If the hammer coral succumbed to an infection, it may have spread to the *Acropora*.

So you have a CO_2 system in the closet eh? I won't touch that one. To answer your question, no, I don't think your lack of success with *Acropora* had anything to do with a shortage of CO_2. The use of CO_2 in reef aquariums is primarily intended for the purpose of keeping a cap on the pH. The CO_2 acidifies the water when administered, so it prevents the pH from rising too high from photosynthesis or the administration of the alkaline solution of calcium hydroxide, a.k.a. "kalkwasser". Since CO_2 is a fertilizer for plants, and is employed in planted freshwater aquaria for that purpose, some marine aquarists (that includes me too) have wondered if it could could be administered to boost coral growth. In fact, it does not work for corals the way it does for plants. The algae in symbiosis with the coral utilize CO_2 from their host's respiration...there is no shortage. Administration of CO_2 for the purpose of fertilization generally suppresses the pH, hindering the calcification process which proceeds most rapidly at a pH of about 8.4. So, the only circumstance where CO_2 administration is beneficial to the reef aquarium is when the pH tends to rise too high (above 8.45) during the day as a result of photosynthesis or kalkwasser addition.

So, why do your *Acropora* die? It amazes me how often aquarists look to their water quality for answers to mysterious illness or death in corals when quite often the cause is predation or improper placement of the specimen. So the aquarist buys all kinds of filters and filter media that aren't needed, switches salt brands, does massive water changes, spends lots of money and time, and still can't figure it out. The location in the tank, orientation to light and water motion, and exact means of placement are very important.

The use of underwater epoxies, described in the book *The*

Reef Aquarium, provides an effective means of placing whole *Acropora* colonies. These colonies are often shaped like little tables or bushes, with living tissue from top to the pedestal-shaped bottom. With epoxy these pieces can be placed so that they are projecting naturally above adjacent rocks from a high point, where they can get adequate water flow and light. Without epoxy, aquarists trying to prevent their $100.00 piece of coral from falling off its perch on the live rock may place it in the crook or valley between two rocks...I have seen this many times in home aquaria and dealers' tanks. The result is generally death of the tissue around the base and lower branches because of shading and reduced water flow. In hardy species this usually proceeds slowly, and the healthy, illuminated tissue from upper branches spreads onto adjacent rocks, fixing the coral in position and allowing it to grow upward, even though the lowest branches have died. In delicate species the loss of tissue may proceed into an infection with protozoans that rapidly consume all live tissue. What one sees typically is branches becoming white and the tissue disappearing or sloughing off at a very rapid rate. I suspect this is what killed your *Acropora*, Simon. You have made an erroneous generalization which, unfortunately, has become commonplace: you called the loss of tissue "bleaching." Ok, when you place a piece of coral in clorox solution the effect is the same, a dead, bleached white skeleton with no tissue on it, so the erroneous use of the term "bleaching" is understandable. Well, this is not what is meant by the scientific term "bleaching" when referring to hermatypic corals. That term means loss of pigment and/or zooxanthellae, which results in a noticeable lightening of color, but not tissue loss. Such blanching (probably a more appropriate descriptive term) is commonplace and results from the corals attempt to adapt, to readjust it's pigment density and zooxanthellae population to best utilize new light and temperature conditions in the aquarium. Corals typically regain natural appearance within a few weeks after a so-called "bleaching event", once they have become repopulated by an appropriate strain of zooxanthellae and altered their pigment density. The administration of trace elements, particularly iodine or iodide, seems to assist in the recovery (Wilkens, 1991). In

Acropora, the tissue is so thin that it can be difficult to distinguish loss of pigment from loss of tissue.

The tissue loss caused by bacterial and protozoan infections is contagious (ie. it can spread to other corals) and it can be very destructive in a short period of time. It most closely fits with the scientific description for "white band" disease in corals. *Acropora* is particularly susceptible to protozoan attacks, as is hammer coral, by the way. Hammer coral is easily cured of infections by dipping the whole colony in freshwater for a minute (which kills the protozoans) and then replacing it in saltwater and flushing the colony with strong water motion to clear excess mucus produced and prevent protozoans from developing large populations. Unfortunately the freshwater dip is not as effective with *Acropora* since *Acropora* tissue is thin and more easily damaged than fleshier *Euphyllia*. When *Acropora* shows signs of protozoan infection, the best remedy is to cut off the affected branches with a good margin of healthy tissue, and then direct a strong current stream over the remaining healthy colony. Of course remove from the aquarium all branches or colonies that show signs of tissue sloughing and the characteristic loose "brown jelly" proceeding as a front adjacent to bared white skeleton, indicators of a protozoan infection. When a whole colony is affected, cutting off small healthy branches and placing them in a separate, clean aquarium with strong water motion can often save them, and new colonies can be grown, so all is not lost.

Is the epoxy a problem? Not likely, especially considering the success with the other corals. Substances leached by soft corals? While there are studies published that link toxic exudates from soft corals to declining health in stony corals, my experience with maintaining both in the same tank has generally been good. I think that protein skimming and activated carbon sufficiently prevent accumulation of toxic substances from soft corals. Should you use ozone? In my opinion, no, and rest assured this is not a missing factor in your reef aquarium. Protein skimming with air only, not ozone, is the best means of water purification. I don't highly recommend turf scrubbers either, as you probably know, but your skimmer seems to have beat your scrubber at nutrient removal, though you might get better growth from it by increasing the light. If you give a turf scrubber a whole lot of light it should still be productive on a closed system even with very low nutrient levels. Be sure to keep up with trace element additions with a scrubber and skimmer working on the system!

On the subject of light, you did not give me the dimensions of your tank, nor the height of the bulb over the water. If anything I suspect you don't have enough light. One metal halide bulb per two feet of tank length is a good rule of thumb. The bulb should be about six to twelve inches over the water. Without knowing how you have your lighting arranged, I suspect that it might be an indirect factor in the lack of success, though I feel pretty confident that placement and protozoan infection is the direct cause for your lack of success. How deep is your tank? where did you place the *Acropora*? Near the top? Generally *Acropora* should be placed pretty high up in the tank to get the strongest light.

Q. Dear Mr. Sprung, Last summer I made some changes to my reef system. I did away with my trickle filter, removed my ozonizer, and removed all types of mechanical filtration. I added an additional 20 to 30 lbs. of live rock, and 2 to 3 inches of live beach sand which I collected from the northern seacoast of Massachusetts. Three months have passed since I made these changes, and my two and a half year old 125 gallon system has shown noticeable improvements. However, I am concerned that I may have overlooked something when adding either the live rock or the "live" beach sand (i.e. parasites). Within the past four to five weeks I have lost a coris wrasse, an algae blenny, and most recently an orange spotted goby. I have no idea why these animals suddenly died. My corals have never looked better and the fish have always looked healthy. Last weekend, however, I noticed something which I have never seen before. One of my fish, a cardinal, has what appears to be some type of parasitic worm embedded just beneath the skin, directly under his right eye. The clearly visible worm is brown and appears to be boring its way towards the fish's brain. I am concerned that my tank may contain parasitic worms that are gradually killing the fish. Although I only have five relatively inexpensive fish, I do not wish to see them suffer. Do you have any idea what this parasitic worm type creature is? Do you have any suggestions for eradicating the parasite? Also, is it possible that the invertebrates are unaffected by the worm? All corals appear to be thriving, and certain species are multiplying.

I am concerned that the beach sand I collected may be the culprit. Could I have inadvertently introduced native Atlantic parasites into a tropical environment? Could the parasites have come from the live rock also introduced last summer? Any information you could give me would be much appreciated. I am extremely concerned over the situation and I do not wish to see matters get out of hand.

Sincerely, Carl Paolucci, Medfield, MA

A. Dear Carl, I imagine you having a dream about your tank: You walk into the living room one morning and all that's inside your tank is one writhing mass of spaghetti. As you turn to run, one little noodle hops up onto the edge of the tank, cocks a "head" toward you in an inquisitive way and leaps in a straight line at your back. There you are screaming aggggh, agggh! as it inches its way toward your ear! You said you were concerned three times in your letter. I suspect this means you are terrified.

Without seeing the "worm" I cannot say for certain what it is. If it is entirely embedded under the skin, it probably is a worm. If it is hanging out with just the head under the skin, then it is more likely a parasitic copepod, a type of crustacean, not a worm. I don't know whether the losses of fish are related to the creature you noticed below the cardinal fish's eye. My inclination is to believe that they might be related, but to suspect that they aren't. (I hope that is a relief to you). Your description of "sudden" loss of several fish does not sound like the result of parasitic worms or copepods. Such parasites cause a slower more agonizing decline in health that would be apparent before the fish died. I suspect first that the addition of 2 to 3 inches of sand may have created a   oxygen plummet that may have asphyxiated some of the fish. How did they look when they died? Did you find them in the morning? Were the gills flared? I am not opposed to the quantity of sand you used, but I just want to warn you that it requires strong water motion in the tank to maintain adequate oxygen saturation when there is a thick layer of sand on the bottom. Without strong circulation it is possible for the oxygen to fall low enough to suffocate the fish directly, or for the formation of toxic hydrogen sulfide to occur, which would asphyxiate them as well. With strong circulation in the tank this is not a problem.

Fish parasites can be introduced with nearly any introduction to the tank, but generally they come in with fish. I am constantly amused by aquarists who never quarantine their fish and suspect the food, rock, or water is the source of parasite problems, never the newly introduced fish! I don't know how proficient you are at recognizing symptoms of fish disease, Carl. I am not entirely convinced your fish didn't die from *Amyloodinium*, probably the most common killer in marine aquariums. Still, you did say the fish "always looked healthy", which suggests not disease but asphyxiation.

What to do now? First, make sure you have enough circulation. The water should be noticeably moving with pretty rapid velocity throughout the tank. This need not be constant velocity...the use of wave timers on powerheads helps eliminate dead spots and pushes more velocity over short bursts of time than could be tolerated constantly by the invertebrates. Second step, if you can remove the cardinal, do so. If he is large enough to take the bait you might be able to catch him with the really tiny hooks available in fishing supply shops...a piece of chopped shrimp on the hook should bring him out...he won't put up much of a fight so don't yank too hard or you'll send him flying across the room.

I'm not certain what course of treatment to recommend without knowing what kind of parasite the fish has. You should check out the article Captive Husbandry of Batfish by David Schleser in *Aquarium Frontiers* Spring 1994 issue. In it he describes the use of the drug praziquantel and fenbendazole for controlling flukes and nematode worms. The fenbendazole can be administered orally, while praziquantel is used as a bath. Also consult the book *Aquariology: The Science of Fish Health Management*, published by Tetra, for additional information about parasite control. As you are aware, you can't treat a reef tank with medication. Fortunately, parasite problems rarely are so problematic that they don't go away if the aquarium is left without fish or with resistant fish. Very seldom does a tank develop a case of the "cooties", don't worry.

I'd like to make a few comments about some of the statements made in an article by Dr. Leo Morin in the March 1995 issue of FAMA. My criticism of the parts of the article do not reflect my opinion of the whole. I respect Dr. Morin's knowledge about water chemistry and the fine reputation of his company Seachem. Still, despite the wealth of well-presented information in the article, there are some comments he made that are, to use his own words, "self serving pseudo scientific gobbledy-gook," and some that are just wrong. The former category, in my opinion, is manifest in Dr. Morin's hypothetical model of the dynamics of nitrification in a closed system aquarium, utilizing versus not utilizing wet/dry filtration. I say "hypothetical" because that is what it is, although one is led to believe that there is some documentation of his claims when there isn't. Furthermore, Dr. Morin uses some confusing definitions that are actually loaded presumptions. To be more specific, Dr. Morin describes the removal of a wet/dry filter as '"removing some nitrification capacity." That definition suggests that the system has lost some ability to deal with nitrogenous waste. In my opinion, it has not as I will explain in a moment. Dr. Morin further; emphasizes the dynamics of his model with a series of questionable statements. He believes that the typical drop in nitrate accumulation that accompanies removal of a trickle filter is a product of "less ammonia ... being formed," and "the concentration of nitrogenous organic matter ... increas(ing)," with "the nitrification of ammonia ... decreas(ing)."

I believe that the latter comment is correct. In my model, the wet/dry filter raises nitrate concentration because it has unlimited oxygen to proceed with the conversion of ammonia to nitrate. It does not offer more "biological capacity"; that is, it does not offer the aquarium any margin of safety over its absence. Just compare the surface area of any media in a 1ft³ box filtering a 100-gallon tank to the surface area contained within the tank in the sand or gravel and highly porous limestone rock.

One of the problems with wet/dry filtration, in my opinion, is this rapid conversion of ammonia to nitrate. What's wrong with that, you may wonder. Two problems are created: First, is that the conversion of ammonia (NH_3) to nitrate (NO_3) involves the liberation of hydrogen ions which results in depletion of alkalinity and pH, making it difficult for calcifying organisms (i.e., corals) to grow. Second, is that the conversion rapidly removes ammonia, the preferred and most easily usable food source for the coral's zooxanthellae, and replaces it with nitrate, the less preferred form of nitrogen which tends to accumulate.

Nitrification of ammonia is faster in a wet/dry filter primarily because of the oxygen availability, but also because the wet/dry filter design employs surface skimming. The surface water has associated with it the nitrogenous organic compounds to which Dr. Morin refers. The wet/dry filter, therefore, should become a site where heterotrophic bacteria develop that convert nitrogenous organic matter into ammonia and carbon dioxide. Morin is correct that the filter has a high capacity to convert these organic compounds to ammonia, but it also rapidly converts the ammonia to nitrate. In the aquarium (as opposed to the dry portion of the filter) there is less oxygen available, only about 7 ppm compared to ca, 20% in the atmosphere pulled through the dry filter. Therefore, in the aquarium without a trickle filter, ammonia is likely to be more available as a food source, even though there is more than enough area on the rocks and other surfaces to handle the conversion of ammonia to nitrate. It happens a little more slowly underwater. Morin's proposed notion that nitrogenous organic compounds will accumulate since ammonia is formed less readily, makes no sense to me. Is he suggesting that the filter is the only place where these organic compounds can be broken down, or that there is more surface area in the filter than in the tank? Neither of these notions are true.

Dr. Morin states, "There are no magic reef bacteria that bypass nitrification and directly remove ammonia and other nitrogenous compounds." The only thing correct about that statement is that what happens does not involve magic. In fact, there are some bacteria that directly consume ammonia and other nitrogenous compounds, but more important than these, in a reef aquarium we have a whole bunch of zoox-anthellae living in the corals, anemones, and giant clams, and they directly consume ammonia and other nitrogenous compounds from the water.

When live rock and live sand are used, as is the practice in modern reef aquaria, we do not, as Morin puts it, "short circuit" nitrification when we remove the filter (external wet/dry filter). The "filter" exists in these living substrates. Lately, there has been wider dissemination by Tom Frakes, Bob Goemans, Sam Gamble, and others, of information regarding the use of live sand and live rock, and their respective roles in the nitrification and denitrifi-cation of the water.

The last difference of opinion I have with Dr. Morin's article involves the comments he made about limewater. First, he states a figure of "a maximum of 270mg/l calcium (under the best conditions!)." The average aquarist is led to accept this as fact, but it is not. Limewater may have at least triple that concentration of dissolved calcium when supersaturat-ed, and much more can be suspended in it before dosing it in the aquarium, where it will dissolve. Further, he asks if anyone has done "the arithmetic" to calculate the quantity of calcium supplied by limewater. Strangely, in the example he gives, he seems to have done the math wrong. There is no refuting that kalkwasser can supply enough calcium to maintain or elevate the level in the aquarium. It. is not as efficient a means of supplying calcium ions as, for example, calcium chloride or calcium gluconate but, in practice, the results with growing corals afforded by kalkwasser are con-sidered best by many aquarists, including me. The reason has less to do with calcium than with other effects of kalk-wasser, including pH elevation, neutralization of organic acids, and precipitation of phosphate. I agree, however, that kalkwasser use does require extra discipline.

Q. I have a 180-gallon reef tank which is in very good con-dition. It has live rock with great pink color My big problem is that the rocks contain multiple *Aiptasia* anemones. I have tried injecting them with calcium hydroxide to no avail; it stops the growth temporarily. My tank has large mushrooms, two tube anemones. and about ten fish. I am desperate and willing to try anything. I have tried peppermint shrimp with no success.

A. I am revisiting the topic of *Aiptasia* because I have new information to share. Old advice suggests using fish that eat *Aiptasia* such as the Copperband Butterfly *Chelmon rostratus* or Raccoon Butterfly, *Chaetodon lunula*. Peppermint shrimp, *Lysmata wurdemani* also will prey on *Aiptasia*, as will some angelfish. These fish may also eat other invertebrates that you don't want them to eat, and when you remove the fish the *Aiptasia* return since the fish merely prune the anemones and don't really eliminate them. Injecting the anemones with chemicals or boiling water works when small numbers of anemones are present, but this method is impractical if there is a plague of them. The best technique was suggested to me recently by John Brandt in Chicago. John noticed that an "*Aiptasia* free zone" seemed to always exist around Elegance coral, *Catalaphyllia jardinei*. He then experimented with brushing the anemones with the tentacles of an Elegance coral and found that after a few such exposures the anemones died. I tried this and found it works well. The coral tentacles should make full contact with the anemones for just a few minutes per day for several consecutive days. Sometimes the anemones are killed by the first contact. Anemones that contract rapidly into the rock may require several "hits." It helps to have a very small Elegance coral to work with, as the anemones can be in really awkward positions to reach. Some may not be possible to control by this method, so, ultimately, a combination of techniques may be employed. Nevertheless, I think the stinging technique suggested by Mr. Brandt is the best general cure for this problem. Other aquarists have since noticed that the Stony coral *Hydnophora excesa* also stings *Aiptasia*. Some specialized nudibranchs feed on *Aiptasia* as well. See *The Reef Aquarium* Vol. I for further information about them.

Q. At one time I had a scarlet cleaner shrimp (*Lysmata amboinensis*) in my tank. When I added my *T. crocea* to the tank, the shrimp was all over it. Thinking it was cleaning it (as the clam remained open) I let it be. After a couple of days I noticed the mantle was considerably shorter. I promptly put him in my hospital tank. The clam's mantle regrew within a week. Thinking I could have been mistaken I tried ,again. The same thing happened so l removed the shrimp permanently. This isn't an isolated thing either. A fellow hobbyist had the same thing happen, only he couldn't remove his shrimp. After about four days the shrimp had completely destroyed the clam. Have you ever heard of this before? I would also like to say that I am a woman— yes there are a few of us out here, contrary to popular belief!

Dawn Harder, Kewanee, Illinois

A. I should hope so! What Dawn really means is that there are far fewer women than men who keep reef aquariums, a fact that I lament.

Yes, I've witnessed this problem with shrimp before, but it does not mean that one cannot keep them with tridacnid clams. There are two possible explanations for the shrimp's attraction to the clams. One involves substances released by the clam that attract crustaceans, serpent starfish, and other potential predators. The other possibility is that substances from your own hands, rubbed off on the clam, draw the shrimp to it and then the clam's own secretions produced as a stress;response to the pestering shrimp, further attract the shrimp in a vicious cycle ending in the death of the clam. Small clams are particularly vulnerable, and they may be attacked even by the otherwise innocuous tiny herbivorous hermit crabs. Large clams can deal with hermit crabs simply by shutting their valves rapidly enough to knock them off. The hermit crabs will literally eat an entire small clam while it is still alive. If you pick up the clam they are attacking, you will notice why they are attracted to it. It smells ! I cannot understand the function of this odor as it certainly serves no beneficial purpose for the clam. It is produced when the clam is stressed, which increases the likelihood it will be attacked at a time when it is most vulnerable, a cruel circumstance. I believe the clam produces the smelly secretion, but perhaps it does not. It is possible that the odor is produced by bacteria attacking the stressed clam.

I have witnessed serpent starfish promptly march over, pick

up and consume a tiny coral fragment or cutting that I carefully placed by hand in the aquarium. Hermit crabs similarly
will pile up on such a fragment, and the weight of them may
knock it over. These creatures are very sensitive to smell, and
substances from our hands can be attractive to them, particularly if one has just been eating. Couple this with the habit
that new additions made by you to the aquarium are most
often food, you should be able to understand why the occasional creature added might be mistaken for food.

Stressed clams often release smelly mucus, and they are
often stressed by the process of being moved to your tank.
Therefore, it is essential to watch them carefully as you have
done, and take steps to prevent them from being attacked. If
the clam had been established already in the tank and you
added the shrimp after it, most likely the shrimp would not
have attacked it. The clam would simply blend into the
"background" of odors. However, if the clam ever became
stressed, the shrimp might then attack it.

A. My friend and I have been in saltwater fish for two years.
We each have a 60-gallon tank with fish only (no live rock
or coral). Each system has a wet/dry filter, protein skimmer,
30-watt 50/50 lighting, basic prefilter, and floss/sponge for
mechanical filtering. On three different occasions (twice in
my tank and now in his) our water has become cloudy with
what I assume is green suspended algae. On my first
encounter, a large 50-70% water change was performed
(along with wall scrubbing and substrate vacuuming). After
this, an algae killer for salt/freshwater was used and the
water cleared over the next week. Everything was great over
the next three months. Green algae began to reappear on
the rocks and corals which decorate the tank.
Weekly/biweekly tank maintenance kept this well under'
control for the next two months until I left for vacation.
When I returned, the green cloud had returned to my tank. I
once again performed my 50-70% water change with algae
killer. However, this time I had two immediate deaths, a Fox
Face and a Naso Tang.

Other fish in the tank (Raccoon Butterfly, Tomato Clown,
and Blue Damsel) also seemed to be affected and stopped
eating. I removed all the remaining fish immediately and

transferred them to a quarantine tank and brought the Raccoon Butterfly to my friend 's tank. (No green water was introduced to my friend's tank: the butterfly was netted into his tank.) I used the recommended dose of algae killer in my tank and left the light off for two weeks. Attached algae died and were removed by scrubbing, but the green cloud remained and, in fact, grew in density (visibility was down to three inches). Meanwhile, after two weeks my friend 's tank is now showing signs of the same green cloud. Ammonia, nitrite, pH, and nitrate are all within safe levels. Phosphate was not tested. We have been using Renew to control phosphate and nitrate. Protein skimming and filter floss/sponges do not appear to have any effect on it. The cloud seems to grow in density with no lighting or fish food introduced to the system.

With heavy pressure from my wife. I am almost ready to throw in the towel and let the green cloud win. Is there any way to either control or cure this green cloud? All the fish stores have no answer to my problem. Jeff Schmidt and Bradley Beming Los Angeles, CA

A. Bradley should be pretty peeved at you for inoculating his tank via your butterfly fish ... what makes you think that the green cloud could not be transferred with the fish? Of course it could. What you have there is an algal bloom, phytoplankton, aka "green water." Three things must occur to make the bloom as successful as yours. First is inoculation, i.e., the algae has to be introduced to the tank in the first place, which is not problematic for the tank, generally. Second, there has to be sufficient light to make it grow ... in my experience these blooms are most common in tanks situated by a window where they receive some natural sunlight daily. I'm willing to bet your tank fits this description. So despite the lights being "off" it did receive enough light. Third, an algal bloom must have sufficient nutrients to grow or it will eventually crash. My suspicion is that you use unfiltered tap water for your evaporation top off. In some areas the tap water is the perfect fertilizer for these blooms, being a rich source of phosphate, iron, nitrate, and other important nutrients. Once a bloom gets started it really doesn't take much to keep it going, as you found out. For example, the slight production of ammonia by larval fish in a rearing tank will cause such blooms when the tank is inoculated with the algae.

So, you still want to know how to cure the problem. A diatomaceous earth filter temporarily installed on the tank will filter out the algae, and clear the water. The D.E. filter should be broken :r down and recharged with new diatom powder at least every two days. This will effectively remove the algae with the trapped nutrients they contain. To prevent the bloom from returning, you need to consider purification of your source, tap or well water. A UV sterilizer of sufficient wattage on the tank can also be used to prevent or cure this problem, but it is not as effective in curing it as D.E. filtration.* I do not recommend algae killing solutions to combat problem algae. When they didn't work for you the first time why did you try again? I'm not certain why those fish died, but I suspect it may have been suffocation. The algae can consume the dissolved oxygen rapidly when not illuminated. It is also possible for these blooms to be toxic, though the surviving fish suggests that was not the case in your tank.

Q. Recently my simple, yet highly automated 1000 L reef tank began to get quite murky. I began to notice over a three day period that the water was getting very cloudy with a yellow tint. During that time I had a heavy schedule, so I only saw it in the early morning or late at night when all was dark. By the third day, I could see things were very critical and I had checked all of the obvious causes and had done additional water exchanges. There is an auto water exchange system which daily exchanges a few liters, so a press of a button can exchange any additional amount desired from the basement holding tank. I went down to the basement where the RO unit and saltwater holding tank is. Although everything seemed okay, I took off the cover of the saltwater holding tank for the auto exchange and found the problem. A large opossum had gotten into the basement through the cat door, got the holding tank lid loose, fallen into it and drowned days before, turning the water into opossum rot. Although I lost only a few fish and one coral, it is difficult to express how much work is required to recover a system from this kind of problem. The system tends to oscillate, screwing up one thing after another.
Sincerely, Alan, Kirkland, WA

*My opinion has changed on this point. I consider a UV sterilizer more effective than a D.E. filter for solving this problem. U.V. sterilizers are commonly used on freshwater ponds to clear green-water algae blooms. They are quite effective for this purpose.

A. What you didn't know Alan is that the opossum had been sneaking in every so often for months to treat himself to a nice relaxing dip in your salt spa. This time he just got a little bit too comfortable in there. Your experience is an excellent demonstration of Murphy's Law: "If it can happen, it will." Readers will no doubt be curious, as I am, why you didn't notice a foul odor in your basement. Perhaps you attributed it only to the aquarium's decline!

More books, less time ...
Those of you who may be wondering where I've been the past several months will note the new book, *Reef Notes, Revisited and Revised.* I have not been taking a break! In addition to working on the journal Aquarium Frontiers and working on Volume 2 of *The Reef Aquarium*, I have started a series of books based on this column, with revisions, after-thoughts, and new information thrown in. So, now you can have all the "Reef Notes" and more, with a subject index as well. The first book in the series, which is now available, covers the columns of 1988 through 1990, and offers a lot of new information in the appendix (to order call 1-800-969-7742). I hope you can pardon my long absence in 1995. I'm looking forward to getting back into the habit of finishing my columns on a more regular basis.

November 1995

Q. Dear Julian, Congratulations on an excellent column! I am writing in to discuss some problems and ideas with you. Firstly, I am having problems keeping my *Goniopora* and *Xenia* corals living. My other corals, including stony corals such as 4 varieties of staghorn, 3 brain corals, several soft corals, one *Euphyllia*, some *Actinodiscus* sp. and *Porites* coral are thriving and showing good growth. My 240 litre aquarium has 2 150 watt metal halides, a Sanders protein skimmer, two powerheads for water circulation, and it is full of live rock. Fish present are a blue tang, yellow tang, percula clown, flame hawk, and a *pseudochromis diadema*.

I have tried moving the corals to areas of more and less light and current to no avail. Both corals are still alive, but have been reduced in size to about 10% of their former selves. The *Goniopora* portion that is still alive has still calcified (its skeleton is higher than the dead component) but still doesn't look as healthy as it did in the beginning.

I have a lot of algae growing on the sand and glass (insufficient protein skimming I think) but there is very little growing in the live rock and corals. Water parameters are: nitrate 0, KH 8dKh, phosphate 0.1 mg/L, pH 8.2. Kalkwasser is added as top up water. Also, do you have any tips on keeping *Tubastraea* coral in this kind of set up or should I avoid it altogether.

I also want to ask your opinion on using CO_2 to a.) reduce the pH of kalkwasser so that it can be added all at once, and b.) whether increasing CO_2 in the aquarium would help stony corals to more rapidly assimilate the calcium? Would this result in faster growth? Are there any other ways to encourage more rapid growth in stony corals?

Earlier this year I had several soft corals spawn at about the same time of year they normally would have done in their native habitat. Is there any way I can safely collect and grow these eggs?

Thanks again to FAMA for a brilliant magazine. I only wish it didn't take so long to get here to Australia!

Regards, Paul Groves, Palmyra, Australia

A. Dear Paul, Are you sure that's all you want to know? Difficulty with *Goniopora* is not so unusual. It is a subject I've covered before in this column and one that has appeared elsewhere in this magazine (see for example Dana Riddle's series of articles on coral nutrition, FAMA April, May, and June 1994). There are many species of *Goniopora* and most do not do well in the long term in closed aquariums. The most common imports, *G. stokesi* and *G. lobata* can do well in captivity, and there are others which are possible to keep and grow, but some *Goniopora* species simply don't survive well in captivity, and the reason is still a mystery despite many hypotheses. One reason for failure with this genus is that it is very prone to infection with *Helicostoma* sp. protozoans that rapidly consume tissue. This is the same problem that commonly afflicts *Euphyllia* species and *Acropora* species. The tissue turns to brown jelly and sloughs off. It is also the most common killer of *Heliofungia* species in captivity. A one or two minute freshwater bath will stop the infection by killing the protozoans, and the coral should be temporarily placed in a separate holding tank with new seawater and strong circulation to prevent re-infection.

Another malady that affects *Goniopora* is more gradual, and fits your description of the coral not looking as healthy as it once did. The polyps don't expand as much, the tentacles are shrivelled. This condition may last years. It is tempting to consider nutritional deficiency, but the long duration makes it puzzling. Irritation by neighboring corals, soft corals, pestering fish, etc. have all been considered too. So has collection damage, boring algae and water quality (see *The Reef Aquarium*, Vol 1). Although any of these things may contribute to decline in a particular example, none seems to be a definitive cause for failure with this genus. I do believe that a nutritional aspect is part of the problem, but I also suspect that lighting plays a role too. The long duration of the condition and the appearance of the tentacles in unhealthy specimens reminds me of the symptoms caused by production of active oxygen in the tissues as a result of photosynthesis. Aquarists have noted that trace elements reverse this condition in anemones and other types of corals, but no study has been done to measure the effect of trace element additions in reversing the decline in *Goniopora*. Of course the symptoms in test specimens must be of the long duration kind, not from short term factors such as pestering fish or protozoan infections. Light plays a role in the development of these symptoms in other corals, and it also plays a role in the development of accessory pigments (which trace elements may also affect) that can help the coral to deal with the light and with detoxifying active oxygen. Dr. Craig Bingman (in press, *Aquarium Frontiers* journal) is investigating the role of green fluorescent pigments in this process.

With respect to your troubles with *Goniopora* I cannot presently offer much advice. I generally recommend avoiding this genus, but you may be one of those people who looks for challenges. You can try *G. stokesi*, which has an increasingly better survival record in captivity. The closely related genus *Alveopora*, which occurs in Australia and therefore should not be too difficult for you to obtain, also has a pretty good survival record in captivity. Most

Alveopora are hardier in captivity than most *Goniopora*, though they may sometimes suffer the same maladies.

You did not elaborate further on your difficulty with "*Xenia.*" Unfortunately, the name has become meaningless lately as dealers are using *Xenia* to describe many different types of soft corals and even colonial anemones! *Xenia* is best given the common names pulse coral, pump-end *Xenia*, or pumping *Xenia*. It is a soft gelatinous coral with eight pinnate tentacles on each polyp that usually "pump" rhythmically, opening and closing as if grabbing something from the water with so many fingers forming a fist and then opening up again to repeat the cycle. It's the kind of coral that makes some aquarists drool, mesmerizes most observers, and stimulates a really wicked case of the "I gotta have it's" in those aquarists who can't seem to find it for sale anywhere, but get an occasional fix by seeing it in an aquarium where it is proudly displayed but, of course not for sale. The pumping action is not for food capture*, by the way, as *Xenia* do not have the means for capturing and digesting prey. They are photosynthetic creatures, dependent on their symbiotic zooxanthellae. The pumping action appears to serve a few functions, including exchange of respiratory gasses and light flashing. It may also aid in the assimilation of dissolved substances from the water, or in the liberation of excess mucus (*Xenia* produce copious amounts of clear mucus).

I must assume that since you said *Xenia* you meant *Xenia*. Difficulty with this coral is a quaint attribute that seems to enhance its sexy appeal and increase its demand. In my experience two factors are primary for failure with it and a few are secondary, but still important. First, in order to really thrive *Xenia* species prefer high pH. I have noted that there is a correlation between the coordination and intensity of pumping, as well as the healthy appearance of the fine pinnules in the tentacles, with pH. When the pH is consistently at 8.2 to 8.4 during the day, the tentacles come together to form a perfect point at their tips. At lower pH values the tentacles become stubby or choppy, and the pulsing is less regular, often uncoordinated, with the tentacles coming together in pathetic twisted attempted clutches or curling outward and not pulsing at all. Another factor in the failure with

*Well, not the typical kind of food capture most people would envision. *Xenia* spp. do not trap zooplankton. What they are catching is dissolved organic material. The copious mucus they produce serves as a "molecular net" that traps passing organic compounds which can be consumed by the coral. See *The Reef Aquarium* Volume Two for more details.

Xenia is letting it grow too densely. *Xenia* grows very quickly when it is healthy. The proud aquarist who finally succeeds with it for the first time invariably makes the mistake of sealing off the aquarium room from all visitors, following an obsessive-compulsive regimen of gestures and duties that surely must be done in order to perpetuate the luck with the *Xenia*, and wouldn't think of touching the colony or even breathing too heavily near it. So of course pruning it with a sharp scissors would be completely out of the question. Within a few weeks or months the colony grows too thick and then "crashes." Sometimes the entire colony is lost this way, though usually a few stalks survive. When the crash produces a "brown jelly" infection, caused by the protozoan *Helicostoma*, the result is often loss of all *Xenia* in the tank. With *Xenia* you "gotta be cruel to be kind" in order to succeed in the long run. The colony must be thinned out periodically by cutting out stalks with a sharp scissors. Placing the cuttings in separate aquariums increases your chances of keeping this coral should the *Xenia* be lost in any one tank.

Some other minor factors that improve success with this coral include temperature and water movement. Generally most species fare best in aquariums at cooler temperatures (74 to 76 degrees) despite the fact that in the wild some species can be exposed at low tide or left in hot pools before the incoming tide flushes them with cool water. Most *Xenia* species prefer strong intermittent water currents. These appear to assist with the shedding of the clear mucus. Finally, the addition of iodide supplements has been observed to enhance the growth of *Xenia*, and other trace elements may also be beneficial to it.

Your trouble with algae on the gravel, Paul, could be solved with the addition of tiny herbivorous hermit crabs that grow no larger than about an inch and actively turn the gravel while feeding on algae. Water currents also help as they may prevent the algae from growing there by tumbling the top layer. The algae on the glass could be controlled with herbivorous snails. The use of purified make-up water curbs the growth of algae on the glass, but the purification also removes potentially beneficial trace elements that might be in your unfiltered tap or well water. As

you noted, increased protein skimming also helps curb
algae growth, so you might try it as well.

Tubastraea species are not so much delicate as demanding.
They are hardy, but require daily feeding in order to thrive.
They do not have symbiotic zooxanthellae. What I recommend doing to make the care of *Tubastraea* manageable is to
use underwater epoxy to stick the coral on the glass or on a
rock a couple of inches below the surface of the water in an
area with strong water flow but indirect light. *Tubastraea* like
strong water currents, particularly in intervals as from a wave
timer. I place the coral so high up because it makes access
easy for feeding it. If it were located lower in the tank one
would have to reach in to feed it or fill the tank with excess
food, which is wasteful. *Tubastraea* will feed on flake food,
Daphnia, Copepods, Krill, Mysis, Brine shrimp and other
shrimp, and worms. You can soak the dry foods with vita-
mins or Selco for added benefit. *Tubastraea* will normally
expand its polyps to feed at night, but the smell of food in the
water will make it open up during the day. If you feed the
coral the same time daily it may "learn" to open even before
you put the food in. I don't know whether this is some form
of training or whether it is a response to chemical cues
released into the water by the fish. It is compelling to consider
that these primitive creatures can have some form of memory
when they don't have brains or much of a nervous system.

The most common problem observed with *Tubastraea* is tissue receding from the skeletons leaving the polyps intact
but the coenosteum between them exposed. The result is
often algal growth on the bared skeleton, and eventual
demise of the coral. While observing colonies of *Tubastraea*
in Puerto Rico recently with Santiago Gutierrez I noticed that
some colonies even in nature showed tissue recession. I suspect that there it was probably due to predation as from
Hermodice (bristle worm) or a predatory snail, but it may
also have other causes. The colonies also were attacked by
boring sponges. Still, they were healthy overall and it was a
treat to see some of them open during the day in the sunlight. In the aquarium tissue recession can be caused by predation, but most often it results from starvation. If you see
this symptom, increase the feeding quantity, offer Selco
enriched food as well as live black worms or chopped

earthworms. Of course look carefully at the coral, particularly at night, to be sure that it is not being eaten by a bristle worm, crab, or snail.

Regarding your CO_2 questions, the use of this gas to reduce the pH of kalkwasser solution so that it can be added all at once sounds like a good idea at first, but it isn't. What the CO_2 does first is react with the calcium hydroxide to form calcium carbonate, which precipitates. Therefore, the calcium comes out of solution and you have a very weak kalkwasser preparation. However, if one continues to add CO_2 so that the formerly alkaline kalkwasser solution becomes acidic, the precipitated calcium carbonate will dissolve back into the water. Sounds good? Well, actually one could achieve the same effect by putting chalk or limestone or coral gravel or other forms of calcium carbonate in water acidified by CO_2, so it makes no sense to start this experiment with calcium hydroxide. Furthermore, one of the benefits of kalkwasser is the elevation of the pH it achieves that gives it a beneficial effect of precipitating phosphate when it is added to the aquarium. Of course the high pH of a kalkwasser solution does mean that it must be administered via a controlled slow dosing method such as an automatic top-off system or a drip siphon.

Don't mistake my explanation above to be an indication about the value of CO_2 use in general. In fact the use of kalkwasser and CO_2 dosing in combination is beneficial, just not the way you proposed it. The CO_2 should be administered to the aquarium, not to the kalkwasser. The availability of CO_2 in the aquarium does enhance the growth of stony corals, so my answer to your second question is generally "yes." This effect of CO_2 availability works in several ways. First, the presence of CO_2 in the water suppresses the pH, enabling the administration of larger quantities of kalkwasser (and therefore calcium) without causing the pH to rise too high. Tall aquariums naturally retain more CO_2 than short ones, and tend to have lower pH naturally. The artificial administration of CO_2 via a calibrated pH control system is an effective means of preventing the administration of too much kalkwasser, because it automatically keeps the pH from rising too high. When kalkwasser is added to an aquarium, the calcium in solution reacts with available CO_2 to form calcium bicarbonate and calcium carbonate. This effectively raises and or maintains carbonate hardness and alkalinity. When no CO_2 is available, as when the plants have removed it from the water via photosynthesis, further photosysnthesis can utilize alkalinity as a source of carbon, so the gained carbonate hardness from kalkwasser addition can be lost, unless CO_2 is made available in the water during the day. This is one potential problem of illuminating algal turf filters during the day when the lights are also on in the aquarium. Having the aquarium and turf filters illuminated in opposite times balances the creation and use of CO_2 and tends to preserve alkalinity. A further growth enhancing effect of CO_2 addition is the fertilization effect on plants, which includes the symbiotic zooxanthellae in coral tissues. Corals obtain nutrition from the fixed carbon leaked from their symbiotic zooxanthellae. The zooxanthellae obtain CO_2 from the respiration of their host. This is a nice balance, but it's kind of like a motor running a generator that in turn is powering the motor. There must be an input of power or eventually the two partners slow down and stop working. The power input can be achieved through either partner. The coral may consume plankton and then respire CO_2, the carbon obtained from the digestion of the organic material from the food. The zooxanthellae may obtain CO_2 directly from the water and thus increase its photosynthetic rate, producing more food for the coral. The copious mucus that corals produce is rich in carbon, and is considered a means by which they rid themselves of excess carbon. If they are throwing off excess carbon, then we have a motor powering a generator that results not only in the perpetual motion of the two, but also in the production of excess power. What is the source of all this carbon during the daytime as the zooxanthellae are rapidly photosynthesizing? It seems it must be from dissolved CO_2 in the water in addition to the coral's respired CO_2.

So, Paul, you should be able to see that having CO_2 in the water during the daytime when photosynthesis is rapidly consuming it should result in more rapid stony coral growth. This can be achieved via artificial administration of CO_2, which must be done very carefully via a pH controlled dosing system. CO_2 availability is also enhanced via fish populations, snail populations, hermit crabs, serpent starfish and other respiring organisms. It is further enhanced when an aquarium has "live sand" with microbial populations that breakdown organic matter (and liberate bicarbonate and CO_2) in the process of denitrification. In short, some tanks may tend to run short of CO_2 during the day and would benefit from artificial administration of it, while some tanks have a natural production of it sufficient to keep a balance with its consumption.

To answer your final question about enhancing coral growth, feeding the corals also enhances their growth. So does careful additions of trace elements. However, the addition of food or CO_2 or trace elements all enhance the growth of algae that compete for space with corals. The balance can only be achieved with the proper quantity of herbivores to keep algae growth in check, and limitation of phosphate inputs that tend to impede coral growth while stimulating algae growth. Protein skimming and the use of kalkwasser also help by limiting the level of phosphate that accumulates in the water. The level you measured in your aquarium is a bit high, Paul, indicating that you could be doing more skimming or adding more kalkwasser or limiting a source of phosphate such as make-up water (a water purifier such as R.O. or deionization would help). Denitrification in the substrate helps as well because it allows feeding without causing accumulation of nitrate or depletion of alkalinity.

Congratulations on the spawning event in your tank. Collecting the eggs from spawning corals is not difficult, but raising them depends on whether they have been fertilized. You can collect them with a scoop or a siphon. Place them in another aquarium with some live rock or gravel from the original aquarium to serve the function of biological water purification. I have occasionally seen soft corals spawn in aquaria and in nature, but always it has been eggs released. It is possible that the male gametes released are inconspicuous or transparent, so I did not observe them, but I'm skeptical of this since other corals, anemones, etc. release cloudy puffs of male gametes, or sperm bundles associated with the eggs. With soft corals all I have ever seen is little sand-like grains. I have never observed them under a microscope to see if any development takes place, but collected eggs I held in a separate aquarium did not develop into planulae.

Well that was one letter with enough material for a whole column.

3

December 1995

For the benefit of readers who may not have seen the Summer 1995 issue of *SeaScope* from Aquarium Systems, Inc., I wanted to mention an interesting article. It contains information about reversal of "hole in the head" and lateral line erosion (HLLE), a subject that makes even the experts stop and listen. Steve Collins, Curator at the Indianapolis Zoo-Aquarium reports that supplementing the diet of captive Atlantic Blue Tangs with foods containing high amounts of vitamin A (initially carrots but then later broccoli) reversed the condition after vitamin C supplementation alone failed to produce improvement. The former diet of the fish had included romaine lettuce, spinach, and other prepared foods. Now their diet is broccoli supplemented with peas and other prepared foods. After eight years in the exhibit, the tangs (and other fish present) are symptom-free. Add this to the list of possible cures or preventative measures for this condition.

Q. I have a problem with my reef tank that I hope you could help me solve. I began my 20-gallon reef tank three months ago and, as of today, I have in it 35-40 lbs. of Indonesian live rock, one Elegance Coral, a Flower Pot Coral, a Fox Coral, a Sebae Anemone, a Bubble Coral, and various soft corals including Mushrooms, Fingers, and Polyps. The fish load include two Sebae Clowns, A Fiji Damsel, and a Firefish Goby. I use four 20 watt Coralife™ 50/50 for the lighting (photoperiod: 10 hours), a Skilter 250 for filtration, and a MaxiJet 500 for circulation within my tank.

The problem I have is with my live rocks. When first placed the rocks in the tank they were a very light beige color and, consequently, the whole tank looked very bright. As time passed, I noticed the rocks were becoming darker and darker until, after 1-1/2 months, they were almost black. I took one specimen out and tried to scrub it with a toothbrush, but the stuff just won't come off; however, it did come off when I scratched it with my fingernails.

Since I wasn't going to go through and clean all of the rocks with my fingernails, I decided to take the tank apart and flip all the rocks upside down so the areas that were not exposed to light are now on top. The tank once again looked very bright as there was no growth of algae in areas not exposed to the

light. I also took your advice and installed 2cm of coral sand
on the bottom of the tank. The rocks, however, are now
becoming dark again. I understand that this must be a form
of algae, but how can I eliminate the problem? I have no
growth of filamentous algae and all corals are doing fine. I
measured the nitrate and it seems to be 0 ppm, I have not
measured the phosphate level. I am adding 1/2 teaspoon
Coralife™ Strontium Plus twice a week and 1/2 teaspoon
Coralife™ Calcium Supplement every other day. Should I
cut back on these since you have indicated that too much
trace elements might contribute to the problem? Even with
the frequent addition of calcium, there does not seem to be
any growth of coralline algae on the rocks. If I use reverse
osmosis to clarify my water, would that help?

Best regards, Michael Yiu, Vancouver, BC

A. So tell me, why didn't you want to clean all the rocks
with your fingernails? Taking the tank apart and flipping all
of the rocks seems almost as much trouble! You never told
me the color of the stuff that bugs you, only that the rock
became darker. Well, okay, you did at least say it was nearly
black, but you didn't say if this was green-black, purple-
black, or brown black. In my experience, Indonesian live
rock is fairly well coated with a variety of dark encrusting
coralline algae and encrusting brown algae. Did these die,
or is it possible that one type has proliferated and you didn't
realize what it was? If you told me the dark stuff was dis-
tinctly brown, with the tenacious, "will withstand anything
but" the fingernail test quality you described, then I would
suspect it either of two alga, one being *Ralfsia*, the other
being *Lobophora*. *Ralfsia* is a dark brown alga that forms
crusts similar to coralline algae. It often spreads to the glass
as well, forming brown circular growths typically about 1/2"
across, but reaching several inches across at times, or covering large areas when the individual circles merge. *Lobophora*
is essentially quite similar to *Ralfsia*, but it tends to form
shingles that grow out from the substrate, whereas the former adheres very tightly and conforms to the shape of the
surface it grows upon. Another similar looking but unrelated
plant is *Peyssonnelia*, a red coralline algae that often does
not calcify the way other coralline algae do. *Peyssonnelia*

typically forms shingle-like growths quite similar to *Lobophora*, but usually dark wine colored. Sometimes they are brown, particularly under intense illumination. Sometimes they have patterns or stripes, and sometimes *Peyssonnelia* encrusts tightly, like *Ralfsia*. Personally, I don't consider proliferation of these three species a major problem. Some people prefer to have pink and purple live rocks, but I find that when there is additionally a mix of brown or dark red from these three algae, the effect is very nice. Sometimes *Lobophora* can become a nuisance, as it is capable of overgrowing corals. It is easily cropped back by hand, however, and it doesn't grow too quickly.

If the darkening color is green, then it might be the rock-boring alga, *Ostreobium*. This alga is common in many marine environments and often proliferates in closed system aquariums. It lends a green stain to limestone. What makes it proliferate is not exactly clear, but since it is a plant, it is likely that availability of phosphate could stimulate its growth.

The supplements you are replenishing are not trace elements. Strontium is considered a "minor" element, which refers not to its importance but to its concentration in seawater (about 8 ppm). Calcium is a major element in seawater, because its concentration is about 400 ppm. Trace elements are very beneficial additions, but they can help stimulate the proliferation of algae when other nutrients are also present. Iron and iodine in particular can have this effect. Iodine especially stimulates brown seaweeds, such as *Dictyota*, *Sargassum*, *Lobophora*, and *Ralfsia*. Don't misunderstand me, I recommend the addition of these and other trace elements.

You asked if you should "use reverse osmosis to clarify (your) water." You meant to purify your evaporation makeup water. If this dark color is a problem alga and you are using unfiltered makeup water, then my answer is yes, it would help. The water you are using probably has trace elements (and phosphate) in it that are assisting in the development of this alga, and filtering them out would likely change the environment in time. It is also likely that the excellent health you reported for your corals is due in part to trace elements supplied by the make-up water. If you purify the water, but don't add supplements, some of the corals may suffer. The reverse osmosis filter should bring the phosphate (if present) to a level that is not problematic. However, if the phosphate level in the unfiltered water is high enough, the filtered water that contains about 10% of the concentration found in the unfiltered water may still have a problematic level of phosphate. This situation requires additional water purification, such as deionization after the reverse osmosis. Generally this is not necessary. The use of calcium hydroxide in the make-up water has a side benefit of lowering the phosphate level in the aquarium's water, thereby tending to promote coralline algae growth and inhibit the growth of filamentous and slime algae. You might give this a try, though it does require a little more effort than your present regimen.*

If the dark color is a sort of five o'clock shadow on the rocks (i.e., a short turf colored red, brown, or green), then the addition of some *Astraea* or *Turbo* snails would help. You should have these in there anyway. Tiny blue legged or red legged hermit crabs also are good at eliminating tough little turf algae, including the common filamentous "hair algae" that you mentioned you don't have.

Q. I once again need your help. Ever since I've been using kalkwasser (Ca (OH)$_2$) as directed on the label with my RO-DI water for make-up of a 3/4 to 1 gallon of evaporation per day, for some reason I cannot get my calcium readings above 300 on any test kit. When I used calcium chloride and the SeaChem products line buffer, my calcium level was always above 400 and alkalinity was always about 5-6 meq/L. Now I can't get it greater than 3 meq/L. Please help. I need your advice as my SPS corals are receding at a tremendous rate.

Sincerely, Dr. Ron Primas, Bookyln, NY

A. I doubt that the recession of tissue you mention is related to your worries about the calcium level in your tank. Nevertheless, I'll address the calcium issue first.

If you follow the directions and allow the milky solution to settle, decanting the clean solution for dosing, you will be providing a barely saturated solution of kalkwasser. If you

---

Something else I sould have mentioned here is the importance of alkalinity in stimulating the growth of coralline algae. High calcium levels alone will not cause the proliferation of corallines. A stable, high pH, which results from high alkalinity, is more important for the corallines than the calcium level. The dosing of kalkwasser at night via a dosing pump and timer helps to boost alkalinity. The use of balanced ionic buffers also boosts alkalinity and stabilizes pH.

store this for any length of time, it will be undersaturated. It is alternately possible to add fresh strong milky supersaturated solution, but this must be done with great caution to avoid impacting the pH too much. The benefit is that you provide much more calcium this way. I would only recommend the procedure of adding milky solution if you have a pH controller. Having a CO_2 system also helps, as it prevents the possibility of causing too-great a rise in pH, allowing the addition of strong kalkwasser. It also helps by supplying the CO_2 which tends to preserve alkalinity (the buffer) when administered in small doses in combination with kalkwasser. Tanks that do not retain CO_2 (short tanks and small ones with few fish) have a problem wherein photosynthesis remove all CO_2 during the day, causing the plants to then rely on other sources of carbon such as the buffering system (carbonates and bicarbonates). Therefore, the pH becomes high during the day as a result of kalkwasser addition, but plummets at night because the plants have removed the buffer during the day and are respiring CO_2 at night, which acidifies the water.* Back to the calcium issue; some aquarists do add a little bit of calcium chloride occasionally to boost the calcium level, while maintaining it mostly via kalkwasser addition. Generally, I find it unnecessary to do this, but some aquariums, particularly ones with low evaporation rates, may benefit from calcium chloride additions.** Remember what I explained earlier, that it is the calcium hydroxide in kalkwasser that counts, not the water. So one may add (slowly!) a strong milky solution to provide additional calcium.

**Administration of kalkwasser at night via a dosing system takes advantage of naturally produced respired CO_2. It also prevents the drop in pH.*

****Balanced Ion calcium solutions are a new and better alternative to the use of calcium chloride.*

In the near future, another method that has been around for a while will become more widely available as an alternative means of providing calcium ions while maintaining alkalinity. The so-called calcium reactor system involves the use of CO_2 injected into a canister containing coarse limestone chips or coral gravel. This system can be less troublesome to maintain and, if designed correctly, it can be safe. If not designed correctly there is a danger of causing the aquarium pH to fall too low. This method does not cause phosphate precipitation, nor does it elevate pH, so it lacks these features that make kalkwasser advantageous. It does, however, provide both calcium and alkalinity and therefore promotes rapid coral growth.

**See My earlier com-
ments. Jaubert's sys-
tem doesn't supply cal-
ium and alkalinity as
effectively as a calci-
um reactor or kalk-
wasser. It supplies
some calcium and
alkalinity as claimed,
but not quickly enough
to keep up with the
growth of corals and
coralline algae in most
reef aquaria.**

January 1996

To set up the above mentioned system, one must have a CO_2 supply, so it is initially expensive to install, though it is not difficult nor expensive to operate. The system devised by Dr. Jaubert of the University of Nice is even simpler and less expensive, but claims to achieve the same end. It employs naturally generated CO_2 in deep beds of coral sand and gravel ("live sand"). The CO_2 produced by microorganisms in the sand dissolves it, liberating calcium and alkalinity. I am currently evaluating the efficacy of this process as described by Jaubert, compared to kalkwasser use and calcium reactors with supplied CO_2.*

Good luck with deciding how to solve this puzzle ... the buffering system in seawater is not so simple.

Q. When I mix my artificial seawater it produces a very white cloudy solution. What am I doing wrong or is there something wrong with the salt?

A. I have heard stories over the years about small quantities of harmless (but insoluble) calcium carbonate clays contaminating batches of salt, but the white cloudiness you described sounds to me like precipitation of calcium carbonate as the water is mixed. This can happen to artificial seawater when it is mixed with very hard freshwater. What kind of water did you mix it with? Was it purified via reverse osmosis or was it taken straight from the faucet? If the water was from the tap, try mixing the salt again with purified (reverse osmosis) water. If it still produces cloudy water, I would call the manufacturer. If you mixed the salt with water purified by deionization, then the problem may be that the source water was very hard, and therefore the product water from the deionization columns still contained very high quantity of carbonate/bicarbonate (alkalinity) even though the deionization removed all the calcium and magnesium. When the salt was put into the water, the excess calcium it contained spontaneously precipitated with the excess alkalinity in the water. These white clouds are harmless, but they do not make a good impression. Try mixing the salt with different source water to determine what works best. Good luck!

Q. I have kept a marine aquarium (fish only) fairly successfully for several years. recently I have thought about adding some invertebrates, but I have used copper (Cuprex II) in the past (over a year ago). Is there any way to make my tank safe for anemones and live coral? Will lots of carbon and water changes do the trick? Do I have to remove all of the crushed coral and dead coral pieces? Is there any ion exchange resin especially designed to remove copper? Is there any inexpensive copper test that is sensitive enough to detect quantities lethal to invertebrates? I would hate to dismantle my tank. I have lots of green algae and haven't had any losses for 10 months.

Thanks, Dave Trepanier, Terre Haute, IN

A. Your secondary questions after your main question make good material for a comprehensive answer to you. My answer, unfortunately, will not be entirely thorough as there are aspects to your questions that go beyond my experience and knowledge of chemistry. Nevertheless I am comfortable in answering you, as I know what you really want to know and can more than adequately address your primary concerns. Chemists out there in the reading audience may wish to add to my comments, and I encourage them to write to me in care of FAMA magazine.

Your main question is whether your tank is somehow unsafe now for invertebrates. My answer is simply that I doubt that the treatment from a year ago would present a problem now, but that depends on the quantity of copper used, as I'll shortly explain, but first I want to cover the issue of persistence in the water suggested by some of your other questions. The copper does not persist in the water. It rapidly precipitates onto the surfaces of calcium carbonate based materials (your gravel and coral skeletons). It also complexes with organic matter in the water. Therefore, at this point (ie. a year later) water changes and use of filter media that scavenge copper from the water would not remove any copper that may have accumulated in your tank. If you used activated carbon or performed a water change shortly after the treatment a year ago, then some of the copper administered may have been removed, if it had not already precipitated.

Putting aside the fact that excess copper is surely not in your tank's water now, you did ask about its removal from water in general. Regarding your question about filter media specifically for the purpose of copper removal, I am not an expert on the subject, but I know that activated carbon is effective. Polyfilter pads are also effective for removal of excess copper from seawater.

Your question branched further as you wondered about sensitive low range test kits for copper, no doubt owing to your mistaken impression that copper is so toxic to invertebrates that even trace quantities could be lethal. In fact, copper is an essential trace element for invertebrates. Only excess copper is toxic. So, your search for this test kit is not a productive endeavor. Measuring trace levels of copper would not help your primary concern about preventing losses to invertebrates in your tank.

Getting back to my original response to you, I may have given the impression that you have nothing to worry about. Actually, that is only partially true. As I hinted, the quantity of copper used a year ago matters as it relates to the quantity that may be "stored" in the gravel and calcareous decorations. This precipitated copper is not soluble at the normal pH range of a seawater aquarium, so it is "locked up." However, the copper is soluble at low pH, and some copper can be released to the water from the substrate when, for example, a microenvironment low pH is created (in a portion of the substrate) by the respiration of microorganisms. It is possible that the respiration of an invertebrate (ie. an anemone) attached to the substrate could liberate copper in the zone where it is attached, which would not affect the water significantly, but could affect the anemone. Boring organisms that secrete acids to dissolve calcium carbonate could also liberate copper ions in the acidic microenvironment they create. As the copper you used is likely to be precipitated all over the calcareous substrate, you can understand the importance of knowing how much was used to be able to answer the question of whether the amount on the substrate could present a problem for invertebrates attached to it.

The growth of algae on the substrate you described is an indication that perhaps there is not much copper there, and odds are you could get away with being lazy and just going ahead with putting some invertebrates in there.

Nevertheless, if I had the choice in the matter, I'd decide to slowly replace the substrate, changing not more than 1/3 of it at a time at intervals of 3 or 4 months, in order to preserve the aquarium's biological filtration capacity.

I imagine that someone thinking about this situation has already come up with a process for treating the substrate (outside of the aquarium!) to liberate the copper precipitated there. This would involve using an acid to drop the pH. The work involved, though not especially complicated, is probably not worth the effort unless the gravel or rocks are otherwise unobtainable to you and therefore worth saving.

Q. Dear Julian, I just have one more question. I noticed that while I'm dosing my kalkwasser the pH rises normally as expected, but the redox drops by about 30 to 40 mV. Why is this occurring?

Thanks, Ron Primas, New York

A. Dr. Ron, Again you ask a good question so again it ends up in Reef Notes. There is a loose connection between pH and redox wherein decrease of pH most often produces a rise in redox and a rise in pH most often produces a fall in redox, as you observed. The relationship is quite loose as one cannot say how much a change in pH will affect the redox potential. Incidentally, temperature rise also may cause the redox potential to drop. Viewing it the other way around, changes in redox do not generally affect the pH directly, just as they don't affect temperature. The addition of hydroxide ions from "kalkwasser," $Ca(OH)_2$ causes an elevation of the pH, and this pH rise causes the fall in redox potential that you see.

This brings up another point that I have discussed before in this column. Aquarists often develop psychological dependency on redox meters to judge the health of their aquarium as if the meter was a kind of performance gauge. Although these meters do serve a useful function, the numbers craziness that affects some aquarists makes me recommend against having a redox meter. I do feel that a (calibrated) pH meter is very helpful, however. The often repeated advice to observe redox values for "trends," combined with the notion that redox is a measure of water "purity" suggests that a downward trend might indicate a problem. If we consider the above example of the relationship between redox potential and pH, then a downward trend in redox value might represent a trend of elevated pH brought about by photosynthesis or the addition of kalkwasser or buffers. So a drop in redox can indicate a beneficial situation, instead of the presumed decline in water quality from accumulation of organic material or the death and fouling of an organism. Of course a dramatic plummet of redox potential is most often associated with decomposition of organic material producing polluted water.

It is ultimately most useful for the aquarist to be able to judge the health of the aquarium by observing the condition of its inhabitants rather than the numbers on a meter.

Q. Dear Julian, I need some advice about keeping reef aquariums. I've had mine set up and running about two years now. Recently I bought your book *The Reef Aquarium* which has given me a much better understanding of reef keeping. However, I would like your opinion on a couple of things which i'm interested in.

First, I use potassium permanganate about once every two weeks to oxidize pollutants or maybe things that are beneficial to the inhabitants. To dose the tank I have a redox meter to let me see how the chemical is affecting the orp. I mix a very minute bit of powder with a gallon of water and slowly drip this into the tank over a period of 24 hours. It normally raises my orp from about 330 mV to 370 the next day. The orp then levels out at 340-360 mV the following days. I use very little carbon in the system. Will the permanganate create excess nitrate from oxidizing these pollutants? I don't incorporate a "living sand" filter as you have suggested in your book. This is due to the fact that it would be hard for me to remove everything from the tank to put the plate, sand and screening in that Bob Goemans described in his recent article in FAMA. I also don't use a sump, but have a canister filter instead. The protein skimmer is a hang-on-the-tank with an Otto 2000 powerhead. The tank is a 60 gallon flat back hexagon. Lighting consists of two 175 watt 20,000K Coralife bulbs. Circulation is accomplished by three power-heads controlled by Red Sea Fish pHarm's controller.

My second question is what do you think about employing a nitrate reducer?...my nitrates run at 30 ppm total.

If you could give me some advice on running my tank with a better system, please let me know. Micro algae is a problem. It's not out of control but it's always there.

Sincerely, Ricky H. Wrenn, Huger, S.C.

A. I include this letter in this column to add to my previous discussion of redox potential. While most applications of redox control involve the use of ozone with a redox meter/controller, there are aquarists who have used potassium permanganate as the oxidizer. Additional information on this subject can be found in books by Albert Thiel.

I have not experimented with potassium permanganate additions, primarily since I don't employ redox measurement. To put it more directly, since I don't use a redox meter to judge my aquarium's health, I don't use oxidants to raise the redox. Other aquarist-authors have tried potassium permanganate and worked out safe dosing regimens. Although I acknowledge that this method is one among many ways to maintain an aquarium, I don't see any advantage to it.

Regarding the microalgae that persist slightly, this would probably be solved by incorporating more herbivores (snails and tiny hermit crabs) to graze it, and improving water circulation. Water quality alone helps to a point, but there is always a need to have enough herbivores to keep algae in check. Strong water circulation prevents buildup of organic detritus that can enhance algae growth. It sounds like your water circulation is fine, though I don't know the flow rate of the powerheads you are using.

Regarding your question about the oxidant creating nitrate, your point is that perhaps oxidation of organic matter containing nitrogen, or oxidation of ammonia might elevate the nitrate level. In your system of slowly dripping the dilute potassium permanganate solution in the aquarium it is unlikely that the effect would significantly raise nitrate. The use of the other oxidant, ozone, in a contact chamber with high turnover would have more opportunity to affect the nitrate level, however. Your 30 ppm nitrate level is primarily a function of nitrification occurring on and in your live rock, with denitrification inadequate to bring the level lower. If you could incorporate live sand I'm sure this nitrate you are worried about would come down substantially or be removed completely.

Considering the simplicity and low cost of incorporating live sand, I can't imagine why anyone would consider expensive nitrate reducing filters. If your system had a sump and you did not want to disturb the aquarium but did want to try live sand I would have recommended putting the sand and plate in the sump or in an attached refugium aquarium. Since your aquarium does not employ a sump, you can only put the sand in the tank or in an attached refugium aquarium located above or behind the display tank and draining back into it. I can appreciate your not wanting to disturb the aquarium, but I think that in the long run it would be simpler to use the sand than to rely on a nitrate reducing filter. The sand works better too.

ebuary 1996

Q. Thanks for a great column! I've been a serious reader for years before I had a reef tank. Now my tank (180 g) is about 2 years old. I just upgraded the skimming to an ETS 800. It's starting to have fewer problems with algae, and I'm beginning to really enjoy it. I have a question about your response regarding *Xenia* in the November 1995 FAMA. On your comments re. *Xenia* pumping, my observations are somewhat different. I have an expanding colony and the daughter colony pumps in a more coordinated fashion than its parent. The two are still attached by a thread of living tissue, but are on two different rocks, obviously in the same tank under the same pH conditions. My tank runs in the 8.35 to 8.45 zone usually due to kalkwasser dosing, and the dKH is about 8. The parent may be crowded. May crowding inhibit pumping? I notice overall that pumping is inhibited by high light and is greatest when just half the number of metal halide pendants are on over the colony. The colony's polyps are stretched out to their greatest lengths when all the lights are on.

If I should be pruning the parent colony to thin it out, then should I prune off one of the "branches?" Or is that too extreme? And as far as re-attaching pieces, what do you recommend to attach with? Rubber bands? Plastic toothpicks? (which I have yet to find). You didn't mention Lugol's solution, as was described in *The Reef Aquarium* as a possible preventer of wipeouts. Do you not believe that? What dose should I be using? I just started adding it to my tank. If it doesn't prevent wipeouts then at least it should be beneficial to my corals.

On an unrelated note, what species of small polyped stony (SPS) coral would you recommend placing in a soft coral tank on its evolution from a soft coral to a hard coral community? Frogspawn? Thanks for your time. I really enjoy Aquarium Frontiers as well. Wish I'd started subscribing to that earlier!

Christian Vye, Rhode Island

A. Small polyped stony corals include the branching ones such as *Acropora*, *Porites*, *Stylophora*, *Seriatopora*, and *Pocillopora*. Frogspawn coral, *Euphyllia divisa*, also a stony coral, is a large polyped fleshy coral. It is a fine addition to any reef tank, provided it has room to expand and grow. The tissue expands at least 6 inches out from the skeleton and sweeper tentacles may stretch 12 inches or more. They like mild water motion best, but periodic short duration strong pulses of water from a powerhead controlled by a wave timer will prevent *Euphyllia* from expanding too large, effectively limiting their space requirement a little at least.

Why "evolve" to a stony coral tank? There is a bothersome psychological tendency among reef aquarists lately to aspire toward the challenge of "a stony coral tank," but I'm confident that once the challenge is met you will miss the (usually) less challenging soft corals that happen to be more interesting and generally more beautiful with their fluid motions. Why people get hung up on creating a soft coral only or stony coral only tank is a bit of a mystery to me. I suppose the "word" is that one must choose either-or because of chemical warfare between soft and stony corals. Nevertheless those aquarists who try to mix a nice population of both usually meet with success. I have always mixed soft and stony corals, and while it's true that one must be careful about providing enough room to grow and not allowing certain soft corals to grow onto or next to stony corals, they can coexist in the same aquarium without problems. The use of protein skimming and activated carbon manages to prevent any harm caused by the substances released into the water by these creatures.

However, that brings up another subject. *Xenia* utilize dissolved organic substances as food. Therefore rapid removal of this food source from the water may inhibit their growth (see my answer to the next letter regarding overskimming). While the primary source of nutrition in *Xenia* is supplied by the photosynthetic products of the symbiotic zooxanthellae, this specialized soft coral also traps organic compounds from the water for food. The copious slimy mucus it produces has been described as a molecular net for capturing dissolved organic compounds. So, one can see that it is possible that water that is very efficiently filtered by activated carbon and skimmed by a protein skimmer could slow the growth of the *Xenia*. I just know that some readers will misinterpret my meaning here...I'm not saying to stop using these filters. On the contrary, they should be used. However, take care not to overdo it, or if you must overdo it, be sure to feed enough to make up for it!

Your observations regarding light and pumping relates to the photosynthetic production of oxygen and superoxide in the *Xenia*'s tissues, and possibly also to the production of copious mucus during the most intense illumination. The pumping tends to provide shade to parts of the polyp (light flashing) in addition to moving the internal fluids. This helps to diminish the potentially toxic effects of superoxide. If the water flow is only slight, the accumulation of mucus among the polyps could inhibit pumping, particularly if the colony is dense, which brings us again to another subject.

Crowding that occurs when the *Xenia* colony grows into many stalks tends to concentrate mucus in a way that can smother the individual stalks or promote protozoan infections that clear out the "forest" like a fire. When the colony becomes dense it is time to prune out some of the central stalks.

On the subject of pruning, one way to thin out the parent colonies without the trouble of trying to attach the loose cut branches is to place thin (dead) coral branches or small pieces of live rock among the *Xenia* stalks. Within days the stalks will attach to the branches and then it is a simple matter to cut the stalks away from the parent colony while carefully leaving the new attachment to the coral branches. The process is, by analogy, like touching an unlit candle to a lighted one fixed in position, and using the newly lighted candle to light another candle and so on. Actual pruning will still be needed once in a while, and I just cut stalks with a scissors. I place the severed pieces into depressions on the rock in an area with very light water motion, or on gravel with slight water motion, or among algae. If there is no water motion, the cut *Xenia* may succumb to infection by bacteria that feed on the copious mucus emitted as a result of the injury. If there is too much water motion the cut *Xenia* will blow away and land behind or underneath a rock, with a tendency to gravitate to the one place where you absolutely could not possibly retrieve it. If it doesn't land there right away the only other possibility is for it to get sucked into a powerhead and blown out shredded, which would not kill it except that after it goes through the powerhead it will then seek that place beneath the rocks where you can't get it. From this scenario it should be apparent that the cut pieces of *Xenia* are best housed in a separate aquarium.

Regarding Lugol's solution, there is a positive effect on *Xenia* growth from the addition of iodine (as potassium iodide, iodine dissolved in potassium iodide, or organic extracts containing iodine). The reasons for the beneficial effect are not entirely understood, and probably are plural. I have been supplementing iodine lately by using a full spectrum supplement* and I no longer use Lugol's**, though I did use it previously and found it to be beneficial.

A fascinating pair of articles by Dr. Craig Bingman in the Summer 1995 *Aquarium Frontiers* covers subjects that relate

*CombiSan
**I do use Lugol's sometimes: I find Lugol's to be beneficial to add for the purpose of stimulating the growth of brown and red seaweeds, so I do add it as well as CombiSan to aquaria in which I want to encourage such plants to grow. Just one drop of Lugol's solution per 20 gallons added weekly is sufficient to stimulate lush growth of the algae. Lugol's is also useful for treating some infections in corals, and has been offered for sale as a "disinfecting dip." Follow manufacturers' recommendations.

to Lugol's solution indirectly. One article describes the effect of activated carbon on light transmission through water, and the other describes the possible roles of green fluorescent pigments in adaptation to UV light effects. Since the carbon removes yellowing organic substances from the water, it has a significant impact on the light spectrum and intensity that penetrates the water. Use of activated carbon can effectively double the intensity of visible wavelengths penetrating to the bottom of a deep tank. More importantly, it can dramatically increase the penetration of UV wavelengths at all depths. Yellowing substances are efficient filters of UV light (that's why sunglasses have a yellow-brown tint). The reason the UV is of importance is that it stimulates rapid photosynthetic production of active oxygen or superoxides (peroxide for example) in the coral tissues by zooxanthellae. Therefore, when the water is very clear the coral must have efficient means of dealing with the toxic active oxygen or have good UV blocking pigments. Dr. Bingman's articles explain this in fine detail. After reading the article about activated carbon it occurred to me (and Dr. Bingman as well, pers. comm.) that one possible benefit of Lugol's solution could be that it is yellow brown in color. Its addition to the tank could provide enough tint to temporarily reduce the penetration of UV light, providing a period of relief to corals that have not yet developed sufficient U.V. blocking pigments.*** Still, I believe the effect of iodine or Lugol's additions on *Xenia* may include more than just UV blocking.

**After testing this hypothesis, on the recommendation of Charles Delbeek, I found that the tint afforded by addition of Lugol's does not persist long enough to provide significant duration of protection against UV wavelengths. Therefore the effect of Lugol's is something it does for the coral metabolically.

Q. I have a 55 gallon reef tank. The only filtration is a protein skimmer. I had two canister filters, but I stopped using them and my tank seems to be doing better than ever without them. I recently hooked an air pump up to my protein skimmer to increase the number of bubbles in the skimmer. My question is, should I be worried about the protein skimmer removing too many trace elements? Can protein skimmers work too efficiently? I don't add trace elements, but instead I do 20% weekly water changes. Please let me know your thoughts on this system.

Also, my tank contains many millipede-like creatures ranging in size from 1/8" to 1" in length. They have legs all along their bodies just like millepedes. They normally just crawl in and around the gravel. Two nights ago when the metal halides went off and the actinics were on I saw several of the millipedes swim by spiralling up to the surface of the water. Most of them were promptly eaten by my clownfish. Do you know what these creatures could be? The clownfish appeared healthy this morning so I don't believe the millipedes are poisonous, but should I try to get rid of them so the clownfish don't eat too many of them?

My tank also has two white scaly creatures that look somewhat like flattened limpets but stay buried in the gravel and only come out at night to feed on algae growing on the rocks. They are about 1" long and seem to have an armored, scaly shell. Do you know what these could be?

Donald Clark, Fort Edward, New York

A. The scaly creatures are chitons, a type of primitive mollusk. If you count them you'll see there are eight scales. Chitons can reproduce in captivity and they are beneficial herbivores.

I'm not positive what the "millipede" creatures are, but I suspect they are just amphipods. Hobbyists write to me all the time about these, and describe them as shrimps, bugs, fleas, or parasites. They are harmless and beneficial. They eat detritus and algae. They are excellent natural food for the fish... don't try to get rid of them!

You asked if protein skimmers can work too efficiently. Well, that depends on the skimmer and how much food and trace elements you are adding to the aquarium. Generally the answer is no. Most protein skimmers lag behind the potential that they could remove because of the rate of water throughput they process compared to the rate of feeding and the rate of production of organic skimmable material by the inhabitants of the tank. However, if the skimmer processes the volume of the tank quickly, and there aren't a lot of creatures in the tank, and the aquarist does not feed or add supplements much or at all, then yes it is possible to over-skim the tank, particularly when the protein skimmer is used in combination with activated carbon that, like the protein skimmer, also removes organic substances and trace elements from the water.

You indicated that you don't add trace elements, but instead do 20% weekly water changes. Personally I think it is easier to maintain the aquarium with trace element supplements, and less frequent water changes, but your method can certainly work.

If you worry about the skimmer being too efficient at removing trace elements, then add some back with a supplement. If you worry about it removing too much organic food, be sure to feed the tank regularly. In my opinion it is best to use a skimmer that could potentially over-skim the tank based on its throughput and efficiency, and to add food and supplements. This way you sort of mimic the dynamic equilibrium that successfully maintains reefs in nature. The filter prevents the accumulation of waste while your feeding assures the tank is not nutrient limited.

Q. One of my customers has a problem with a large colony of *Acropora* that is losing tissue at a rapid rate. Do you have any suggestions? Freshwater dip?

Dave , Commonwealth Pet

A. Dave called me with this question, which I had already answered partially in the December 1995 Reef Notes, though the issue was not out at the time he called. What I told him was that the tissue loss was an infection caused by protozoa or a combination of bacteria and protozoa. Although freshwater dips are quite effective in halting the progress of such infections in fleshy corals such as *Euphyllia*, in *Acropora* I have found that freshwater dips are only slightly helpful, and the infection usually returns. Dave sounded a little discouraged by that so I assured him there was a solution to the problem... to break it up! While there were still healthy branches left on the colony the customer could easily fragment branches unaffected by tissue recession. These branches should be placed in other aquariums and glued to the substrate with underwater epoxy. I explained to Dave that with *Acropora* it is more important to maintain the species, not the specimen. Fragmenting the coral and placing the branches in as many different aquariums as possible assures the longterm survival of the species in captivity. The small branches quickly grow into colonies well adapted to their new environment.

The remaining portion of the original whole colony that had the infection should be removed from the aquarium carefully since the protozoa are able to spread to other corals. Place it in a container underwater and lift it out of the aquarium with the water. If one has many aquariums, one could place the infected remains of the colony in isolation in a small aquarium to see if any tissue survives. Even if no tissue survives, within a week or so the protozoan bloom will have crashed and the base can be used as live rock. It is even possible to attach a few of the surviving fragments with rubberbands or epoxy and have them regrow tissue over the old base.

References

Bingman, C. (1995). The Effect of Activated Carbon Treatment on the Transmission of Visible and UV Light Through Aquarium Water. Part 1: Time-course of Activated Carbon Treatment and Biological Effects. *Aquarium Frontiers*. 2:3. p 4.

Bingman, C. (1995). Green Fluorescent Protein: A model for coral host fluorescent proteins? *Aquarium Frontiers*. 2:3. p 6.

March 1996

Q. Dear Julian, I finally set up my first marine aquarium this past summer after contemplating and planning for about three years! I've "created" a 20" x 17" x 15" sized ecosystem to fiddle around with before I dive into a bigger one later on, at least 100 gallons.

I've built in it a sub sand filter that was described in the '95 FAMA to the letter. It was very easy to do. On top of that I've built another two platforms of PVC and eggcrate so that it tiers down a half inch lower than the back.

Here are my questions. I see these filamentous white threads that have a whiplike action that grabs particles of sand to build a tube for itself. Will they harm the *Xenia* in any way? At night just before the Actinic lights turn off, little flat undulating worms jet crazily around the tank. What the heck are they? I've only seen one bristle worm and I've disposed of it. Could they be swimming bristle worms breeding? Once in a while I get this golden coloured jelly that appears on the tips of the rocks. Once a week I suck out about 1 to 2 cc's of it out. What is it and what can I do to get rid of it (if I have to)? Finally, I've developed minute pockets of gas in the upper 1/2 inch layer in the sand. The author of the article does not mention any gas buildup in the sand bed...could it be nitrogen gas or hydrogen sulfide or methane? I see the cucumber ingest sand in the area of the gas buildup but it doesn't seem to bother it.

Sincerely, Wilson S. Choi, Toronto Canada

A. Dear Wilson, You obviously spend a lot of time looking closely at your reef tank. Your thready creature was described in *The Reef Aquarium* in the "What is that?" pages of the appendix. The little two tentacled tube builders are called Spionid worms. They are harmless detritivores.

The crazy worms you see swimming at night I described in a past column. I used to observe them at dusk at the surface of the water in Biscayne Bay near my home when I was a growing up. At the time I called them "vroom worms" for obvious reasons...they really zipped along! They are the reproductive structure of a polychaete worm. Actually they are like reproductive individual worms that bud off of the worms still remaining in the substrate. This phenomenon is called epitoky and the "crazy worms" are called epitokes. Have no fear, they aren't bristle worms. Nereid, syllid, and eunicid polychaete worms commonly employ this reproductive strategy. The epitokes swarm in a reproductive frenzy in the water, shedding their gametes. When they swarm in a reef aquarium like you have observed the usual result is that they and their gametes are caught and eaten by the corals.

*It could also be a type of cyanobacteria that grows in clean low nutrient water with strong illumination. I have had these show up in my own aquaria and find that tangs and herbivorous hermit crabs usually eat them. Some places, such as the tops of rocks or corals at the water surface, cannot be reached by the herbivores.

The golden coloured jelly you are siphoning out is probably a type of dinoflagellate*. Hopefully it will remain a minor component of your reef community. When dinoflagellates bloom they can cover and smother sessile invertebrates and they may be toxic to herbivores. I've explained in this column and in *The Reef Aquarium* that the use of kalkwasser seems to keep them in check.

The gas bubbles you see in the sand are probably not nitrogen gas. Nor are they hydrogen sulfide or methane, since you would not have to ask if they were, as they have a distinctive disgusting odor and the formation of visible bubbles of either would surely result in you being aware of them. What you see there are probably bubbles of oxygen. Generally the high intensity illumination over the sand results in the development of a variety of algae that penetrate the upper layers. The algae occur quite deeply along the side glass walls because there they have more light. It is along the glass where you notice the product of their photosynthesis-- oxygen.

It is certainly possible that nitrogen gas bubbles can be produced in the sand as a result of denitrification activity there. The observation of bubbles emitted from the sandbed was described in numerous articles by Bob Goemans in Marine Fish Monthly magazine over the past few years and subsequently by other authors describing natural nitrate reduction as Bob calls it, or the "Jaubert system," after the person who patented the technique of utilizing an elevated sandbed specifically for denitrification. Bob Goemans observed that bubble formation occurred in proportion to the amount of food added to his aquarium.

Q. I have a 55 gallon tank I'm setting up. I'm 19 years old and now have a 20 gallon marine tank. It's home to about 25 pounds of well developed live rock, a Keyhole Angel, Percula Clown, Yellow Tang, and a Watchman Goby. The 20 gallon tank has been set up for about a year and a half.

My question is, in setting up my 55 gallon tank, I was thinking of using wood to simulate a pilon on a pier which will enclose the uplift tubes for my UG filter and in turn be home to my anemones, barnacles, and other viable tenants.

I have never heard or read about anyone using wood or the effects of wood in a marine system. So, if you could, please elaborate on its use in a marine system. Thank you.

Yours Truly, Oliver Jones, Felton, DE

A. While many marine aquarists these days can't remember what a lift tube is, being so accustomed to wet dry filters or reef aquariums run without external biological filtration, you have a neat idea for a different kind of tank using the old undergravel filter method. Your idea of concealing the lift tubes this way is creative. Sounds like something we'll see sooner or later coming as a plastic molded piece to slide over the lift tubes.

I've seen spectacular displays at the Monterey Bay Aquarium, where they maintain pilings encrusted with strawberry anemones, sponges, barnacles, mussels, and other marinelife. These are open system aquariums, so otherwise delicate filter feeders are thriving on the pilings. The effects of the wood on the water are not a concern since the water is flushed continuously.

Regarding the wood, I'm sure there are some types of wood that could be toxic, particularly if they have high resin content or are treated or stained, but generally waterlogged pieces that you can find in a river, or drift wood commonly used for decorating freshwater tanks can be used in saltwater. The reason why people avoid using wood in marine tanks is that it can stain the water. The accumulation of tannins leached from the wood can be controlled to some extent by the use of activated carbon. In a small tank it is possible that a large piece of wood could affect the pH, driving it down. In a 55 gallon tank the amount of wood used to conceal the lift tubes would not likely have a significant affect on the pH. You can expect it to rot with time. If you are worried about the wood falling apart with time, you could consider concealing the lift tubes with a stack of rocks instead, each with a hole in the middle like a doughnut. By the time you attach marinelife to the rocks you will not see much difference between them and the hollow log you proposed to conceal the lift tube. Alternately, if wood is the only thing for you, you could apply a clear epoxy coat to the dry piece of wood to protect it from rotting. Allow the epoxy coat to completely dry before putting the wood in the tank.*

*It may be necessary to use rock to weigh the wood down as the epoxy coat prevents water from soaking the wood.

Q. Dear Julian, I have a couple of questions for you. The first is about a fish-only aquarium, but I would like your opinion. Sometime in the future I would like to set up a fish-only aquarium with a capacity somewhere around 500 gallons. My question is, what would be the best biological filtration for an aquarium of this type and size? I would like to stay away from wet/dry filters because I've read that they become nitrate producers. I know live rock would work really well but I don't want to have to shell out the cash for the amount of rock required to properly filter an aquarium of this size. I was thinking more along the lines of a fluidized bed filter with live sand as the aquarium's substrate for denitrification. What is your opinion on this? Do you have any other suggestions?

The other thing I wanted to ask you is what Volume Two of *The Reef Aquarium* is going to cover. Thanks very much and keep up the good work.

Ken Wald, via Internet

A. Dear Ken, The live sand is not simply a denitrification zone, it also functions as a nitrification filter, converting ammonia to nitrite and nitrate. So, with sufficient sand you have a good biological filter already. Then the rocks are only supplemental biofilters. You don't have to shell out the big bucks to fill your 500 gallon fish tank with live rock. I recommend that you build a reef structure with porous limestone rocks. You can add some live rocks to provide a seed culture of various bacteria and microorganisms, and also coralline algae.

So, do you need an external biological filter. In my opinion, no, you don't if you have sufficient sand and rock in the aquarium. I would recommend a protein skimmer, however, as supplemental filtration to handle the dissolved organic load produced by heavy food inputs typical of fish-only tanks. Fish systems utilizing reverse flow undergravel filters combined with mechanical filtration are an old standard that works, but typically produces low pH and low oxygen levels. Standard flow undergravel filters have the disadvantage of collecting detritus that eventually impedes their function, but they are cheap and easy to install, and when properly maintained have quite a high capacity.

Your comment about wet dry filters concerns me as it suggests that you don't fully understand their function. Yes, wet dry filters produce nitrate. That's what they are supposed to do, convert ammonia to nitrate. That is the principal function of any so-called biological filter. Complete biological filtration of course involves the conversion of nitrate (or nitrite) to nitrogen gas and nitrous oxide. The reason wet/dry filters get such a bad rap is that they are most efficient at converting ammonia to nitrate, since they operate with such a high availability of oxygen and receive the surface skimmed water that is often rich in dissolved organic nitrogen containing compounds, precursors of ammonia. Submerged forms of biological filters are also potential nitrate factories, but this depends on water circulation that provides them with oxygen and exposes them to the nitrogen containing compounds. The advantage of submerged biofilters is that under the right conditions they may provide denitrification sufficient to limit the nitrate accumulation. In wet/dry filters the high flow rate and availability of oxygen generally produces a situation where nitrate accumulates faster than it is eliminated by denitrification.

I have not experimented with fluidized sand filters, so I cannot offer first-hand experience with them. I have heard a lot of praise regarding their function from people who use them. It sounds like they work well as biological filters and have the distinct advantage of never clogging with particulate matter. One disadvantage I can see, depending on the design, is that if they are designed to hold water in the event of a power failure, then extended power failures could produce a situation where hydrogen sulfide would build up in the column filled with water and settled-sand coated by active, oxygen consuming strains of bacteria. One could then have hydrogen sulfide flowing into the tank upon starting the filter up after an extended (more than 12 hour) power outage. If the column mostly drains in the event of power outages, the sand should naturally remain damp in the closed cylinder for several days, and oxygen would not be in short supply, so there would be no chance of hydrogen sulfide formation and the bacteria would remain damp enough to survive. My comments here are not based on first hand experience with fluidized beds but on theory and my experience with shutting off canister filters, which do differ significantly from fluidized beds.   filters typically have accumulated organic detritus that greatly assists in the rapid oxygen depletion by bacteria in the small water volume during a power outage. Fluidized beds lack the organic accumulation, but do have the bacteria population capable of depleting the oxygen in an extended power outage.

Volume 2 of *The Reef Aquarium* is still in progress. It will feature biology, taxonomy, and identification and care of soft corals and anemones, including zoanthids and coral-limorphs. There is additional information about some newly available stony corals and about giant clams, diseases, and parasites. It will also feature new information about filtration, lighting, etc. and another tour of tanks around the world*.

*The new information about stony corals, clams, filtration and lighting did not end up in *TRA* Volume Two. They will be included in future books.

Addendum:

Last month there was a question regarding the removal of copper from aquarium water. I mentioned activated carbon and other media, but forgot to mention two other products specifically developed for the purpose: CupriSorb, from SeaChem Laboratories and Mega Media Copper Remover from Aquarium Systems, Inc. Sorry about the oversight.

May 1996

Q. Julian: My 2 1/2 year old reef tank owes much of its success to you and I must thank you and those at Aquatic Specialists in Knoxville, TN, along with my local "reef friend" John Progno for all the help I've received. Someone should point out that knowledge is a great key in this hobby, and the more you know about reefs and their biology, the simpler and easier and cheaper it is to own and maintain a reef tank that is truly a thriving, growing, and astounding testimony to one of nature's most beautiful creations. Everyone that sees my tank wants one and I've gotten three other "reefkeepers" off to a start- it's addictive!

Question time: My yellow tang seems to "graze" off the *Tridacna* clams' mantles. The clams have warmed up to this behavior and no longer close up, but what the heck is this fish doing? It's not food that he's picking off them, it's more that he skims the mucus off the fleshy colorful part facing the light.

Question two: All my water changes and supplements are dripped in. Whenever I do so, (and usually only when I do) my *Hydnophora* sp. coral exudes a white spaghetti-like substance from its polyps, usually at tips that would appear to be growing points. This stuff usually compacts back in towards its point of origin. This is a totally different growing method than I have observed in other corals if, in fact, it is a growing method. Are you familiar with this?

Question #3: I've had great success and then eventual failure with bubble/bulb tip anemone (*Entacmaea quadricolor*). My solitary large bubble tip thrived for approximately 2 years. It got large (approx. 16 inches diameter) under my halide/Actinic lighting. My Tomato Clownfish (*Amphiprion frenatus*) spawned under its tentacles for its last 13 months of existence, constantly nipping its tentacles back from the spawn site. This seemed to have a negative impact on the cnidarian. The anemone eventually shunned the light and fish and moved under the rockwork to die. Since then, two more bulb-tips have done the same. Incidentally, everything else in the tank (including *Acropora* corals) are growing just fine. Another anemone of the same type was in with the original anemone, given to a friend's reef and has now divided.

It has been suggested to me that large populations of mushroom anemones (*Actinodiscus, Rhodactis,* etc.) may be a detriment to anemones such as *Entacmaea quadricolor.* If so, I have these reproducing all over the tank... want some?

Incidentally, I have baby fish from the spawning pair. Thanks a million, Julian. This is the first tank I've ever owned and you helped immensely!

Sincerely, Gary Majchrzak, Rochester, NY

A. Dear Mr. Marcj, Machrz, Muzak, Ma, er, um, Dear Gary, Glad to know you are happy with your reef, and I'm even more thrilled that you are sharing your enthusiasm and getting more people hooked.

Regarding your first question, what makes you think that mucus isn't food? Remember that kid on the bus back in elementary school who used to... well, you know? When clams (and corals) are healthy and their zooxanthellae are photosynthesizing, they convert carbon dioxide from the water and from the hosts respiration into organic compounds. One way of getting rid of excess carbon is to shed mucus which is rich in carbohydrates (ie. a decent source of energy for who-ever eats it). Often the mucus also has bacteria or other microorganisms associated with it, which may also be nutritious to the consumer. Sometimes, when the host is ejecting excess zooxanthellae, the mucus may have some of these trapped in it, which would interest your herbivorous tang.

Regarding your second question, the white strings coming out of your *Hydnophora* are acontia filaments*. These are often emitted as a defense mechanism when the coral senses a change in the environment. If you see the filaments only when you are dosing something, you may be dosing too quickly. The acontia are digestive mesenteries that pack quite a punch. They are often thrown out over an adjacent coral as a means of attack, to kill the adjacent tissue and prevent encroachment by the neighbor. Acontia filaments are also involved in the growth process, sort of, for certain corals, including *Hydnophora*. What the corals do is to clear the substrate of competitors in advance before they spread new growing tissue over it. This can clearly be observed when corals grow on glass. They frequently put out acontia to kill the algae on the glass immediately adjacent to the growing front of tissue.

*Oops. wrong. They are mesenterial filaments. Acontia are a *type* of mesenterial filament associated with certain types of sea anemones. It is therefore incorrect to call all mesenterial filaments acontia.

Regarding your third question, I can only offer some possibilities. First, some forms of *Entacmaea quadricolor* frequently divide in nature and in captivity. This is a means of asexual propagation, which you are familiar with if you've been observing your mushroom anemones... they do it too. When one of these anemones is going to divide it typically withdraws and appears to be dying. I am convinced that many anemones undergoing this process are extracted and thrown away by their over-concerned owners who fear the anemones have died. I occasionally get a letter from an aquarist who left the "dying" anemone alone and suddenly discovered two where once there was just one.

During the process of dividing the anemone is more vulnerable than usual. It is possible that a bristle worm hidden in your rockwork is consuming the anemones at that time. Bristle worms can actually stimulate the anemone to divide by taking a big bite out of it. I suspect you may have a big bristle worm in there. Have a look at night with a flashlight.

Another reason an anemone might withdraw is that it is getting too much light (intensity or duration). In this case the anemone would typically open up for a few hours and then withdraw. That does not sound like what happened in your case. This could happen when changing the light source or if one uses activated carbon after not using it for several months. The carbon removes yellowing substances from the water and can dramatically increase the light penetration, particularly UV light.

I've never before heard of the connection with mushroom anemones causing other anemones harm. I suppose it is possible, but for now I doubt it. Congratulations on your success with the clownfish!

Q. I have been trying to solve a mystery now for 4 months regarding my 75 gallon reef tank. Every time I put a brittle starfish in the aquarium, within a few hours all his legs will drop off and within a day his body turns to mush, or he'll get a hole in the middle. I must have gone through a dozen brittle stars of different varieties from different suppliers.

They all do the same thing. After I had cycled the aquarium, however, the first brittle star lasted about a week before his tentacles began to drop off, and two weeks when he began to develop holes in his body.

First we thought the live sand in my aquarium was the problem, that it was slowly releasing a toxin. Also, by the way, I must have gone through some 60 *Astraea* snails, and 3 sea cucumbers (the ugly kind) during the first 3 months. The snails would fall off the glass, on the sand and seemed not to get up. We got rid of the sand and we finally thought we licked the problem. Seven of the snails seemed to do fine, and the one sea cucumber left is still doing fine. During the next month I made several water changes (about four- one 35 gallon water change and three 10 gallon water changes). Even before this I did numerous water changes. Then yesterday we put 2 new brittle starfish in there and the same problem occurred again (apparently the sand wasn't the problem). They were healthy in the pet store, and I watched them feed on squid while they were there.

I don't know what could cause this. By the way the brittle stars lose their tentacles and turn to mush right in front of my eyes. Nothing seems to be attacking them.

These are the average water parameters in the aquarium: pH 8.2-8.4, specific gravity 1.023, nitrite 0 ppm, ammonia 0 ppm, nitrate below 20 ppm, inorganic phosphate near 0, calcium 350-400 ppm. Copper- undetectable, Temp 76-78 °F

I use Coralife Scientific Grade marine salt and always make sure the new water parameters match the aquarium water. The freshwater is purified with the Tap water purifier by Aquarium Pharmaceuticals. The equipment includes: Two 40 watt Actinic 03 and one 175 watt 5500K metal halide, wavemaker with 2 powerheads, 27 inch protein skimmer made by Sea-Thru, Hydrothruster-Q main pump, redundant wet/dry filter with bioballs, no prefilter used.

As far as the tank inhabitants go, I have 1 Flame Hawk, 1 Yellow Tang, 3 Seabae Clowns, 1 Diamond Watchman Goby, 2 Fire Gobies, a few small blue and red legged hermit crabs, 5 small Sally Lightfoots (they leave when they get too big), 2 Coral Banded Shrimp, 1 Colt Coral, 1 Open Brain Coral, some mushroom anemones, 1 Bubble Coral, 1 gorgonian. All seem to be doing fine and look healthy. I feed the fish every other or three days and have some romaine for the tang.

There is about 80 lbs. of what the dealer called coralline encrusted base rock, and an additional 50 lbs of what he called finishing rock. Some of the base rock seemed to be nothing more than encrusted marble that weighed a lot. The rest of the base rock looked Coquina rock, that looks like compressed shells, with some macroalgae looking like grass growing on it. This rock, including the finishing rock, came from the Gulf of Mexico.

The brittle stars were the first thing I put in the tank after the rock had cycled. There was still some nitrite but a nitrate reading was undetectable. I did not add anything else until a few weeks later, but the brittle stars were already dying. When I added the *Astraea*'s most did the same; they closed up, turned over and would die.

I slowly acclimate the tank inhabitants using the drip method. Every time they would die I immediately checked all water parameters which seemed fine. Could there be something in the tank causing a false nitrate reading? Oh yes, the tank windows get a lot of green algae on them quickly (within three days they are covered).

Also knowing that phosphate might not read properly, I have used the phosphate sponge just to see if it has an effect.

I hope you can help me with a solution because i think I have tried everything else, asked everyone else, and read everything else (I have *The Reef Aquarium, Reef Notes,* and *The Marine Aquarium Reference*). What have I overlooked?

Thank you for your time, Marcel Heitlager, Ft. Payne, AL

A. Tough one. Hmmm, there are some possibilities that I can decant from your story. I had a similar question several years ago in this column, and it can be found in *Reef Notes Revisited and Revised* Volume 2, which will be available in June 1996. An aquarist had a problem with snails dying while everything else was doing well. This is similar to your situation. The aquarist thought that the problem might have something to do with the fact that he had put some rocks from his back yard in the tank. In the original column I told him it was possible the rocks had some kind of pesticide sprayed on them that affected snails. This was a long shot, but possible. In *Reef Notes Revisited and Revised* Volume 2 I added the comment that it is possible that there was a toxic dinoflagellate blooming in the tank. If you look at the description of these in *The Reef Aquarium*, Vol One, you will notice the comment that the toxic effects include that "snails ...roll over, stop eating and die." This sounds like your description. While no effect on serpent or brittle stars is noted in either book, there are references to another echinoderm, sea urchins, dropping spines and dying during dinoflagellate blooms. It is intriguing that you noted yet another echinoderm, sea cucumbers, were affected in your tank. So now there are at least some snails and one sea cucumber doing well but the brittle stars still die. That makes the dinoflagellate toxin seem less likely, but it is still possible. You mentioned a green algae that rapidly coated the glass, which is not unusual in a new tank, particularly if there aren't many snails, but I am curious about what's happening on the rocks. You never mentioned what is growing on them now. Dinoflagellates form gelatinous sheets and strings that trap oxygen bubbles. Do you see that in your tank? Control of dinoflagellates, if they are the cause, can be achieved with the regular addition of calcium hydroxide solution, as described in *The Reef Aquarium.*

As I was reading your letter I had a hunch that perhaps you were performing a prophylactic freshwater dip on the brittle stars, which could injure them sufficiently to cause this problem, but by your description of the careful acclimation procedure you use, that hunch seems incorrect. This leaves little else for possibilities, considering the bizarre circumstance that the stars just crumble right before your eyes... For a moment I thought that maybe you might be emitting an invisible laser beam with your gaze, but that seems highly unlikely too, eh?

What's left then? Your description of the live rock was good enough to convince me it was collected near shore (Coquina and green grass-like algae are typical shore residents in your area). That helps me a little, because it affords the possibility that something in one or more of the rocks could be toxic. Sometimes coralline encrusted reef rock is smooth and pale, but not when when it comes from the Gulf of Mexico. Your statement that the rock looked like marble is interesting. Sounds like it is fossilized limestone, which is ok, though it can be pretty dense and heavy, as you noted. Since the rock seems to be from near shore, there is the possibility of some kind of piece of metal could be imbedded in one of the rocks. It is possible that one of the marble-like rocks is really concrete, with metal inside. This is a long shot, but it is possible.

Another possibility, if it were just the brittle starfish you were having trouble with, is that the species you are trying to keep do not fare well in captivity. I doubt this is the problem in your case, but I though I'd mention it while we're on the subject. While most serpent and brittle stars are quite hardy, some species are delicate and do not fare well in captivity. Brittle stars, which have spiny legs, are never got a reply from this hobbyist whether any of my advice helped his situation. However, I have an additional observation mention here. I have seen these symptoms affecting serpent stars in my own aquaria during so-called RTN events. "RTN" stands for rapid tissue necrosis, a type of infection that affects small polyped stony corals. I have observed that when the corals start losing tissue the serpent stars often drop portions of their legs. So it seems possible that the condition can be caused by an infection with virulent strains of bacteria (believed to be *Vibrio* sp.). See *The Reef Aquarium* Volume 2 for additional information.

generally more delicate than smooth-legged serpent stars. One of the delicate brittle star species commonly lives inside tube sponges of the genus *Callyspongia*, and it is probably never collected for aquariums. Another oddly delicate serpent star lives in the Gulf of Mexico, and is extremely abundant in seagrass beds near shore. Both of these typically fall apart in captivity exactly the way you described. The reason remains a mystery. Since you live on the Gulf of Mexico, I thought it was possible that your dealer had obtained one of the more delicate species. Your comment about having tried different types from different suppliers seems to rule out that possibility.

Though I'm sure it is not the problem in your case since you seem to be so careful, it is possible to have these symptoms in brittle stars if they are stressed in transit after you bought them. For example, if the ride home in the car involved a stop at the grocery store and the starfish stayed in the car and got too cold or too hot, by the time you acclimated it and put it in your tank it could fall apart. Another possible cause of these symptoms is ammonia. In a newly established tank with live rock it is common for there to be a high ammonia level before the live rock is fully cured. Your tank has been set up long enough for that to have come and gone, so I know ammonia is not your problem. However I thought I'd mention it so that other aquarists who have experienced the same difficulty with brittle stars might consider the possibility. Brittle stars and serpent stars do not tolerate high ammonia levels, which can cause them to drop legs and fall apart.

All I have discussed here are possibilities and, looking at my comments I feel I did not give you much of substance to work with. As I said, yours is a tough question. What do I suggest now? I think you should try sand again and get some new live rock, which you should hold first in another tank for a few weeks, of course, to avoid fouling your tank. The old rock could be used later in another tank, and it would be interesting to experiment to see if the trouble with the brittle stars is associated with that rock or independent of it. Let me know what you find out.

I am writing this column in March 1996 and the latest buzz in reef aquarium conversations is calcium reactors. At one time not so long ago the term calcium reactor brought to mind a device designed by Alf Nilsen, which employed a magnetic spinner to mix calcium hydroxide with freshwater fed into a cylindrical reactor. Prior to the widespread recognition of that system for adding fresh-mixed kalkwasser, there was another device that was called a "lime reactor." It employed carbon dioxide administered to a reactor chamber filled with chips of calcium carbonate. In the USA the only systems available several years ago were made by Tunze, though there was also a Dupla CO_2 reactor that could be used this way. The increased recognition lately of this system, I think, can be traced to two individuals in Germany. First, a couple of years ago in the journal DATZ, Mr. Rolf Hebbinghaus of the Löbbecke Museum and Aquazoo in Düsseldorf wrote an article about a system he built using Eheim canister filters filled with coral gravel, through which he administered CO_2 and passed a slow stream of water from the aquarium. The effect of the CO_2 dissolving the calcareous gravel is a supply of calcium, alkalinity, and some CO_2 to the aquarium. Hebbinghaus's article demonstrated the success he was having with his large reef aquarium using this method to maintain calcium and alkalinity. In addition to the article from Hebbinghaus, Daniel Knop, an author and aquarium industry manufacturer, introduced a compact "kalkreactor" system and promoted its use widely. Now the rumor among the internet surfers is that kalkreactors (of several different manufacturers) have taken over Germany. Well, that is a little bit of an exaggeration, but it is true that several manufacturers including Dupla, Aquamedic, Tunze, Knop Aquarienechnic and others have built systems and promoted them, and that they are gaining widespread acceptance and affording good results. In the meantime aquarists there are continuing to use kalkwasser and other methods, though of course many are trying kalkreactors alone. For a review of these systems and the advantages of kalkwasser vs. kalkreactors vs. the addition of calcium chloride and buffer, please see the two part article by Alf Nilsen and Dieter Brockmann that appeared in the summer 95 and Fall 95 issues of *Aquarium Frontiers*. In adddition there are also remarks by Bob Stark and Craig Bingman regarding the use of balanced ion calcium and alkalinity additions, and I even have a comment or two in there. Coupled with all of this discussion is an excellent review by Bingman of kalkwasser's ability to precipitate phosphate and maintain low phosphate levels in the aquarium water.

Q. I have been reading your column in FAMA since I subscribed to the magazine 1 year ago. I have also bought your book, *Reef Notes Revisited and Revised*, and follow your advice always. I'm planning to build a denitrification sand filter in a 10 gallon tank as a sump connected to my main sump. My set up is a 50 gallon reef tank, 175 watt 5500K MH pendant with two 30 watt actinic supplements. I have hard corals, soft corals, polyps, usual reef tank stuff. The sump has a Red Sea Skimmer standing beside it and one pump for the skimmer and another for the water return. A chiller is in line with the main pump to keep the water at 75 degreesin summertime.

I would like to make a Jaubert system sand tank without putting sand in the main display tank. In your Reef Notes book you describe a system that sounds simple to make, but I have a few concerns. Here goes my questions:

Is a 10 gallon tank big enough for this 50 gallon reef? How deep should the upper layer of live sand be? If I use live sand on the bottom layer, would creatures be trapped under the screen? Should I use a 1" high plenum? Do I need lighting for the sand stirring creatures or can they live in the dark? Do I need any shelters for the creatures, rocks or whatever? Brittle stars, blue-legged hermit crabs, etc. are good sand stirrers, I've heard, what about gobies? Don't they need some sort of light cycle? How fast should the circulation be? Slow? Should I use some sort of mechanical filter in this sand tank? What do the stirrers do for food if filtration is used? Do I need an airstone in this tank or just water from the display tank? I am planning to run the water from the display tank to the sand tank, then into the main sump and back up to the display. I seem to have much of the system in my head, but I need further advice from a professional. Does all of this sound good to you or do you have any other ideas that will make this project a success. I want to bring my nitrates down very low and do not want to put the sand in the main tank.

Thank you, Sanford Harper

A. I don't know why you are opposed to having sand or gravel in the main tank, but I'll just accept that and say that yes, your plan will work. A 10 gallon tank would be large enough to bring the nitrate level down for a 50 gallon reef tank, depending of course on the amount of food you put in there. if you had 3 or four big groupers or eels and lionfish eating a pound or two of food per day, you would need a bigger denitrifying bed. The use of protein skimming does help lower the load on such a system too, by removing organic nitrogen containing compounds before they are converted to ammonia by heterotrophs.

Yes, the plenum beneath the sand should be about one inch high. You asked how deep the upper layer of sand should be. I have done some calculations and determined that a thickness of 3.547691872 and 1/2" is optimal. This will require constant adjustment as the sand stirring creatures move the sand around and it dissolves. That should keep you busy! OK, so you were serious with your question, I know, so I'll really answer it. For this sump, a sand layer of about 4" thick will work well. In your planned system you actually don't need to have two sand layers with a screen between them. That design is only intended to prevent sand sifters from digging too deeply, and is best employed in the display tank. Sand sifters are most useful in heavily illuminated sand beds. They prevent algae from coating the bottom. I'll answer two of your questions at once here. You don't need light for this 10 gallon sump denitrification filter and, therefore, you don't really need sand sifters. Since the water will be flowing from your reef tank that contains live rock, the sand will become populated by numerous worms that will aerate it and move it around a little but not too much... without any effort on your part. It happens all by itself, if you just let it. One or two serpent stars and a few blue legged hermits could be useful to catch and eat any food that flows over the overflow feeding the sump (no mechanical filter, Ok?). Some brittle stars, which have spiny legs, will move the sand around, making the screened off second layer necessary, so in this sump you should use only smooth legged serpent stars or employ a screen to isolate a layer of sand about 2-1/2 inches thick over the plenum.

Now, it certainly is possible to illuminate this sump and include gobies. live rock, snails, and just about anything you can think of. In that case, you have what is called a refugium tank. It was my intention in volume one of *Reef Notes Revisited and Revised* to offer this possibility as a simple and interesting way to build a reef system that maintains very low nitrate levels. A word of caution: one must be certain to design the system with large enough drains and strainers to prevent creatures from getting trapped in the plumbing! Use big bulkheads and large diameter pipe.

Since you have another (main) sump in line after this 10 gallon denitrification sump (a good arrangement), you will notice that detritus settles in the main sump. So, the main sump becomes a settling filter. You can periodically siphon out the excess detritus from the main sump.

Finally, You asked about airstones and water flow. You don't need an airstone here unless you really want salt creep below your tank. Since your sump will be fed the water from your overflow, it will probably be seeing about 200 gph or more flow through (I am guessing this as it is average for a 50 gallon tank). If the water enters the sump through a large diameter pipe (for example, 2") it will be diffused enough to prevent the sand from being blown around. The flow through this sump and the depth of the sand are parameters that affect the oxygen level in the sand and hence the effectiveness of this sump as a denitrifying filter. You may have to play with the flow a bit to get it to work best for your system. In my opinion the turnover should be fairly high, but the velocity of the water entering this 10 gallon tank should not be high, as it would disturb the sand too much and prevent the required lower oxygen levels through it. You could split the drain water from the overflow to feed directly into both sumps, with ball valves on each leg to regulate the flow, but it would probably be unnecessary to do this. In your planned system, a flow through of 200 to 300 gph would not be too fast as long as it is not from a hard pressure stream.

Q. My question pertains to possible agression between different *Acropora* spp. My divisions were obtained from

Tropicorium in Detroit, as I am writing this, the animals are growing quite fast, and will soon be touching one another.

Will different species react negatively towards each other? Will *Acropora* spp. sting *Pocillopora* spp. and vice versa? I have read your book cover to cover and feel I know what's going on in the hobby, other than coral agression, as I have never witnessed it in my reef. (yet <g>)

I know the day will soon come, and I want to be ready.

Sincerely, Curt De Mars

A. Dear Curt, In my experience some *Acropora* can touch and some cannot. There is a range of reactions. One is a stalemate, where they fuse at the point of contact and neither encrusts over the other. More commonly one will encrust and kill its neighbor. Occasionally, contact by another species of *Acropora* results in a fatal sting, so the affected branch immediately dies. The death of the injured tissue may produce a "brown jelly" infection, caused by millions of protozoans eating the tissue and zooxanthellae. Such infections rapidly spread and consume healthy tissue, and they can spread to adjacent colonies.

Contact between *Acropora* and *Pocillopora* also produces a range of results, usually a border of dead skeleton with algae on it between the species in contact.

Because these branchy corals grow so quickly, the potential for stinging and tissue encroachment is only one aspect of competitive interactions. Another is shading of its neighbors by the fastest growing species. This is easy to manage in the aquarium by periodically pruning the branches. With many *Acropora* spp. it is essential to prune the branches since they continue to grow upwards and shade their own lower branches. The result can be that the lower portion of the colony dies, and if the branches reach the water surface they form a flat "micro-atoll." This is interesting to observe, but if left unchecked the only living tissue will be a small ring around the top edge, and this can easily be lost to an infection or to low tide in the event of a power outage. It is best to prune the colony periodically to maintain it in a branchy form below the water surface.

Q. Is it possible for a fish to recover from a problem with the swimbladder? In other words, when a fish gets in trouble and begins to float upside down is it possible for it to recover? Thanks.

Jim Hoover

...And a similar question...

Q. We have an Imperator Angelfish with a swimbladder problem. It is possitively buoyant and it has been that way since it arrived one week ago. is there a safe way to remedy the situation. Thank you for your time.

Lisa Bruneau, Aquamain's Fish World

A. Many of the fish collected for aquariums are caught below 30 feet deep. Upon being brought up to the surface their swim bladder, a bouyancy regulating organ that holds air, expands. This depends on the depth where the fish lived and the species of fish. Some fish are able to vent the excess air. Most cannot. The collectors use a hypodermic needle carefully inserted into the anus to literally pop the swim bladder. Slight pressure on the swolen abdomen then sends air bubbles out. This is a minor injury for most fish and although their buoyancy may be off a bit for a couple of days, they normally recover. For certain species this procedure is kind of hit or miss, and if the collector is not especially experienced, the result can be an infection. Such infections seem to always make the fish positively buoyant.

Treatment of this condition is not often successful, but not always hopeless! Sometimes the condition corrects itself without intervention by the aquarist. This is most often the case if the fish is only slightly buoyant and is able to eat and pass feces. When the fish is floating upside down looking at you and saying, "I've fallen up and I can't get down!" it will not recover without intervention.

Here's the tough part. There is no way I could advise you the proper way to pop the swimbladder of a particular fish because each fish is different, depending on species and size. If my memory hasn't distorted the tale, I recall hearing about a positively buoyant Leafy Sea Dragon from the Dallas World Aquarium being "brought down" with the help of some time spent in a decompression chamber. If we all had one at our disposal, it would be helpful for this condition! Nevertheless, it is necessary to relieve the immediate symptom to reduce the stress the fish is under. This will involve the use of a clean sterile hypodermic needle inserted into the fishes anus while gentle pressure is applied to the abdomen to release the air. It is best to perform this procedure in a shallow tray (such as a rubbermaid dishpan) filled with water from the aquarium. In lectures Martin Moe Jr. has recommended a procedure he used to calm adult angelfish when strip spawning them. A clean dark towel soaked in the saltwater and gently folded over the fish serves to calm it or at least render it less frantic. In my experience, Moe's technique works very well, so I would use a towel in this plastic dishpan of water. As far as how to insert the needle, I cannot make a recommendation here. I suggest trying to contact a marinelife fisherman from Florida, for example (many of them advertise in *FAMA* magazine). If you can find someone with experience using a needle to pop the swimbladder, mention the type and size of the fish to get a proper recommendation.

Often the condition is associated with an internal bacterial infection. Therefore treatment with antibiotics is helpful (though the air must be released first to allow the fish to swim normally and feed). Unfortunately the current state of the art in therapeutics at the hobby level is somewhere between the stone age and the dark ages. The availability of effective antibiotics is poor, and the dosages and recommended treatments are not widely available nor widely known. This will change, hopefully soon, with the effort of organizations like PIJAC, or possibly the AZA or MASNA. There has been talk about implementing regulation of therapeutics used in aquariums, and some regulations have already been implemented, particularly as they pertain to aquacultured fishes. For now I suggest hobbyists consult the book from Tetra Press called *Aquariology Master Volume: The Science of Fish Health Management*, edited by Dr. John Gratzek and Janice Matthews. It offers good directions for treatment of fish diseases, and recommended drugs to use. Your pet dealer may be able to help you obtain the right medications, but if he can't, it helps to know a veterinarian who can.

In my experience if the fish is able to feed and behaves normally after it has been relieved of the excess gas, it has a 50:50 chance of recovering, its main obstacle being the possibility of a systemic infection. If it does not feed and rapidly develops more gas in the swimbladder, the case is hopeless and the fish should be destroyed.

Gee, that's an awfully sad way to end this column. Well, what can I say, fish die. It's too bad they can't be propagated as easily as corals. We have come to the point now where it is commonly realized that corals are a heck of a lot easier to maintain than fish!

uly 1996

Q. I was wondering what would be the best way to get rid of bristleworms. I know that there are certain fish that eat bristleworms and I was wondering which fish are best for this. Does the *Pseudochromis dutoiti* eat bristleworms, and what exactly does a dutoiti look like and where is it from?

Thank you, Mark Haas

A. Where have I heard that question before? No, I have not run out of questions to answer. I put this question in the column because it reminds me to mention a couple of things. First of all, yes, the fish you refer to does eat bristle worms, though the name you use is a common mis-identification. The fish commonly sold as *P. dutoiti* is actually *P. aldabraensis*. These fish are very similar, differing only by the quantity of blue striping, and by their origin. *P. dutoiti* is found along the African coast from Kenya to South Africa, whereas *P. aldabraensis* occurs from the the Aldabra islands north to the Arabian Gulf.

I wanted to mention that tank-raised *P. aldabraensis* are available now from C-Quest, an aquaculture facility in Puerto Rico that has been supplying them to dealers and distributors for a couple of years already. An interesting feature of the tank-raised fish is a markedly reduced aggression. Wild caught *P. aldabraensis* are MEAN. They usually do not tolerate others of their kind in the same aquarium and, as they grow, they tend to lose tolerance for some of their tank mates. This creates a little bit of a dilemma for the aquarist since the big specimens are absolutely stunning with their contrast of neon blue and orange, but they have a terrible habit of beating up on less aggressive species and they are pretty difficult to catch in an established reef tank. Fortunately the tank-raised fish have a much better disposition and they are just as gorgeous as wild-caught fish.

What you really wanted to know was how to manage the bristle worms. Bristle worms can multiply explosively in reef aquariums, particularly when there is a thick bed of sand or gravel on the bottom, as is common now that aquarists are recognizing the benefit of "live sand". The worms serve a beneficial function because they eat detritus and, as they burrow they help to aerate the substrate. So, as many aquarists have noticed, the small bristle worms that tend to multiply in the sand are not all that bad. The really wicked ones are called *Hermodice carunculata*, and they grow very large (up to a foot or more) while they feast on your corals and anemones. The small bristle worm species generally do not harm corals or anemones, but they do pester or kill small tridacnid clams placed on a sand or gravel bottom. If the clam does not have a rock or shell base to cover and protect its byssus opening, the worms have a clear shot at it and they may kill and consume the clam.

The banded coral shrimp, *Stenopus hispidus*, also eats bristle worms, and it is possible that other *Stenopus* species do as well. So if you are trying to control the worms with a natural predator, you might try banded coral shrimp.

There are also worm traps available from your dealer that are very effective at reducing worm populations. A combination of predators and trapping can easily reduce the numbers of worms in a heavily populated substrate, so that ultimately the predators alone are able to keep the population in check. As I mentioned before, small bristle worms do perform a beneficial substrate turning effect and they eat detritus. Aquarists are overly paranoid about them, I think. In my experience the only danger they present is to small tridacnid clams or clams placed directly on the sand with no rock to protect the byssus opening.

Q. We are doing a project on *Cassiopea* jellyfish and want to know how to take care of them and their tank.

Merry Goodman

A. *Cassiopea* are commonly called the "Upsidedown Jellyfish", and they are the only jellyfish that you are likely to see offered for sale in a pet shop. They are easy to care for if you know their requirements. Like clownfish host anemones and reef-building corals, these jellyfish harbor symbiotic zooxanthellae algae in their tissues. Therefore it is essential that you provide strong lighting for them. Jellyfish are not compatible with powerheads, powerfilters, or overflows, so they can only be maintained in an aquarium without devices that will suck them out or chop them up. The environment where they live is calm shallow mangrove lined sand or mudflats. One can sometimes see them blow by in the current in a channel adjacent to the shallow flats, but in general these jellyfish are restricted to shallow, calm, protected waters, where they sit on the bottom facing their tentacles up to collect the light, and periodically flipping the edge of their disc, which pumps water over the tentacles.

The purpose of this pumping is manyfold. The typical explanation is that these jellyfish trap plankton to supplement the food produced by their zooxanthellae, and the pumping helps to pass more plankton over the tentacles. These tentacles pack a potent sting, so there is no doubt that they are effective at trapping food. Nevertheless, in my opinion they don't require much feeding if they are given strong light. I have seen exhibits of them in which they are fed brine shrimp nauplii to simulate their planktonic food. This works very well, though I think the quantity of brine shrimp required can be significantly reduced if the aquarium is strongly illuminated. It is also possible that these jellyfish trap organic compounds from the water. Other "pumping" cnidarians, the soft corals of the genus *Xenia*, are known to trap organic compounds from the water, and it is possible that the pumping assists this process or prevents them from becoming fouled by the compounds they are trapping. In any case the pumping circulates new water over the animal, which assists in the uptake of dissolved nutrients from the environment.

Another purpose for the pumping could be gas exchange. Since the jellyfish live in quiet waters, the pumping water motion effects sufficiently vigorous circulation to prevent a shortage of carbon dioxide during the day when the zooxanthellae suck it up from the water immediately adjacent to the host. At night the pumping prevents the animal from depleting the oxygen in the water layer around it.

The pumping could also serve another function, light flashing. Light flashing or strobing is achieved by waves passing over a bed of algae. As the algae sway to and fro, they are exposed to the light and shaded from it. *Cassiopea*'s tentacles are packed with symbiotic zooxanthellae and these tentacles look just like upright seaweed. When they are greenish in color they are nearly identical to the common sand dwelling alga *Avrainvillea*, which lives in the same zone as *Cassiopea*. I'm sure that this affords some protection via camouflage. Sometimes the tentacles of *Cassiopea* are blue or purple. This is an indication of the development of UV absorbing pigments, which protect the jellyfish in the shallow, intensely illuminated zone where they live.

To create a perfect aquarium for *Cassiopea* I would use a wide tank ideally, and maintain it only partially full. The water height would be about six to eight inches, over a sand bed that could be just a thin layer on the bottom or a thick live-sand bed over a plenum as described previously in this column. I would use a metal halide light to simulate the intense light they receive, though a row of fluorescents, partcularly H.O. or V.H.O. could also be used. If this were my tank, I'd plant a few seeds of the Red Mangrove, *Rhizophora mangle*, in the sand and include some of the sand dwelling algae like *Udotea*, *Penicillus*, and *Avrainvillea*. For water motion I would use just an airstone. It is possible to use a powerhead with low output for water motion. The powerhead would need to have a sponge cartridge on the intake to prevent the jellyfish from being sucked up and the outflow would have to be sufficiently weak or diffused to prevent shear damage to the jellyfish if they pass by.

Q. I have a 50 gallon reef tank with live rock and a trickle wet dry filter. I use water purified by reverse osmosis and D.I. resin. I'm confused regarding the use of carbon. I was using it continuously and the water was very nice and clear. I was advised by several experts to stop using carbon or only use it a few days per month because of possible depletion of trace elements. Since I stopped using carbon the water is not as clear. I add trace elements to my tank once a week. What should I do? Is it harmful to use carbon continuously? I usually put a bag of carbon in the sump or overflow box.

Sincerely, Joseph Rozas, MD., St. Augustine, FL

A. Dr. Rozas, if somebody told you not to keep a dog because it depletes dog food, or not to leave the house-plants out in the open because they would dry up, or to quit exercising because it causes you to burn up more calories, possibly requiring that you eat more food, would you follow the advice? If I told you that live corals deplete trace elements would you remove them too?

People have many opinions about the use of activated carbon, as I've explained before in this column. In my experience there is no harm done by continuous use of activated carbon, but of course I add trace elements weekly. It could be that when trace elements are added infrequently the continuous use of carbon would deplete the water of them so much as to cause symptoms of deficiency. This might occur, for example, while one is away on vacation for several weeks. In that case it might be wise to avoid placing fresh carbon in the filter just before a trip.

I think that at least some of the symptoms attributed to trace element depletion could be the result of the carbon's ability to remove yellowing substances from the water. Craig Bingman's article in *Aquarium Frontiers* described this effect (see Bingman's article in *Aquarium Frontiers'* Summer 1995 issue... if you are having a deja-vu experience, no worries, I did refer to Bingman's article in a recent Reef Notes column). When carbon is used intermittantly, the water becomes clear intermittantly and yellow intermittantly. The change in water color produces a dramatic change in the intensity and spectrum of the light in the aquarium. The sudden increase in intensity and in penetration of ultraviolet light after carbon use can affect corals and anemones severely, and it is likely that the symptoms produced have been attributed to trace element depletion. One thing which has not been explained is the fact that trace element additions to the aquarium seem to cure symptoms (such as bleaching) that occur as a result of the change in light penetration. It might be that the addition of these trace elements affects the light penetration (UV light in particular)* or it might be that some trace elements are involved in detoxifying active oxygen produced by photosynthesis under strong UV illumination.

*I have seen no evidence that light penetration can be affected by trace elements. I thought that Lugol's iodine might afford a temporary yellow stain to the water that could block UV, but in fact the color from normal dosages of Lugol's does not persist long enough to offer this protection.

So, my advice to you is to use the carbon, and add trace elements on a regular schedule. You mentioned that you sometimes put the carbon in a bag in the overflow box or in the sump. It is better to locate it in the sump. If you place it in the overflow box, the carbon may tumble in the bag, causing it to become pulverized, which allows carbon dust to pass out of the bag... not a desirable situation. In addition, locating it in the overflow box will increase the rate at which the bag becomes clogged by debris, necessitating frequent washing of the bag. When you locate it in the sump, make sure it is not possible for the bag to get sucked up against the pump intake. Locating the carbon in the sump where water flows over it without being forced through it will achieves the desired effect of removing the yellow from the water. You may replace the carbon when you notice the water is becoming yellow again, which is usually after about six months, depending on the amount of life in the tank.

It is interesting to consider the use of ozone for clarifying the water, as an alternative to activated carbon. This method is not always as effective as activated carbon (see Spotte, 1992) and it is perhaps best utilized as an alternative to carbon in really large public aquarium exhibits for which the quantity of carbon required is not practical (Delbeek and Sprung, 1995).

Q. Dear Julian, In *The Reef Aquarium* on page 526 you list vermitid snails/ sessile snails. I've tried to get rid of them by picking them off manually. It didn't work! I need your advice. How do I get rid of them for good?

Thanks, Joe Marchese

*Note correct spelling
is vermetid: I originally
spelled it incorrectly in
this column and in TRA
vol. One!

A. I had to look back at page 526 to try to understand why you got the impression that vermetid* snails were something you were supposed to remove from the tank. They aren't. Vermetid snails are harmless inhabitants of live rocks, and their reproduction in a reef aquarium is a good sign that the aquarium has become well established with populations of beneficial microorganisms. The section on p. 526 is entitled "What is That?" and was intended to show some common reef aquarium inhabitants that aquarists often wonder about. Very often aquarists see things that they can't identify and they either worry themselves sick about them or they reach in and pull out the creature(s) to prevent possible problems with them later, before they know whether the critter in question is good or bad. On p. 526 Charles and I explained that vermetid snails are sessile snails that feed by means of a mucous net that traps bacteria and particulate matter. They are often mistaken for worms. They form hard calcareous tubes and multiply prolifically. In case you didn't know, sessile means that these snails don't move about... they are attached to the rock or glass or plumbing. Perhaps the fact that we did not emphasize that they are harmless made you think they were harmful? The only potential problem caused by these sessile snails is that when they multiply prolifically they may form thick colonies in the plumbing, which can restrict water flow. Ok, there is another bothersome thing about vermetid snails. When they form colonies on the rock they make the rock painful to pick up since their sharp tubes easily puncture skin.

Q. Dear Julian, We have a mushroom leather---- (common names are so dependent on your locality, are there mushroom corals and mushroom leather corals or are they one and the same?) *Sarcophyton trocheliophorum*, that has just today developed a very small, pitch black spot on the edge of its head (face?) near one of the polyps. Any ideas about what it could be? Are we in trouble?

Paula and Larry Shipman

A. Are we in trouble? You and Larry are in BIG trouble Paula, BIG BIG TROUBLE. Why? I don't know, I just thought I'd be dramatic for effect. I agree about the common name stuff. The name mushroom leather coral generally refers to *Sarcophyton* species, of which there are many. Mushroom coral is usually used as a common name for *Fungia* species (a type of stony coral) or for *Discosoma* species (which are corallimorpharians). The top part of the *Sarcophyton*, which you called the head is where the polyps are located. It is called the capitatum*, which means head, not face, so you were right the first time.

*Wrong. It is called the capitulum, which is the mushroom-like head that contains the polyps.

This blemish on your *Sarcophyton*'s head is not a freckle, pimple nor sunspot. It isn't a chocolate chip either. Your description of it occurring at the edge of the capitatum and that it was pitch black is good enough to convince me that it is a patch of necrotic tissue (a.k.a. dead tissue). If the *Sarcophyton* is otherwise healthy this little spot will just fall off, no worries. If the *Sarcophyton* is recently imported and therefore not well established, the necrosis could spread like gangrene. In that case the best thing to do is to cut out the black spot with a sharp scissors and be sure to place the colony upright in a strong current stream.

You might wonder what would cause such a necrosis in a small region in a healthy colony. Generally an isolated black spot like this is caused by a neighboring coral stinging the *Sarcophyton*. Have a look at night to see if a nearby bubble coral, *Plerogyra* sp. or a *Favia* sp. is sending out long sweeper tentacles. If that is the case, it may be necessary to move one of the corals or to place a piece of live rock between the corals to block the sweeper tentacles. Some soft corals may also sting other soft corals, so check to be sure that a neighboring soft coral is not rubbing the black spot. In the meantime, a baster could be used to blow off the spot if it is really small.

There is a slight possibility that what you are seeing is actually a patch of cyanobacteria, as in black band disease. In that case I recommend using a baster or a light swipe from a toothbrush to remove the alga, which should not be left in the aquarium.

References
Delbeek, J.C. and J. Sprung.1995. *The Reef Aquarium A Comprehensive Guide To The Identification And Care Of Tropical Marine Invertebrates*, Volume One. Ricordea Publishing, Coconut Grove, FL. 560 Pp.

Spotte, S. 1992. *Captive Seawater Fishes Science and Technology.* Wiley-Interscience, New York, NY 942 Pp.

August 1996   One long letter

Q. Dear Mr. Sprung, I've been reading your material for quite some time and would like to say thanks very much. Everything in my tank is just a-ok, (eh-ok!)

But I do have a few questions. I have been keeping gorgonians for some time and am learning their taxonomy. (there isn't much in-depth info out there that I can find anyway). Referring to Nov. 94 FAMA, K.I. Minor's Article on Florida gorgonians leads me to believe they are Holaxonians. I have a purple gorgonian that obviously to me loves light. I've taken four cuttings that were 3 cm when cut (the first one in Nov. '95) that have easily grown to between 12 and 15 cm each. They have a central skeleton. The polyps are brown and lightly fluoresce. I've seen this species in many documentaries but cannot find it in any books. It's not shiny, its branches are about 8-10 mm in diameter, and the polyps are fairly large, depending on their placement. Tentacles from tip to tip can reach about 6-8 mm. Would you have a name? Closest I can figure is either a Plexaurid or *Eunicea*(?).

Secondly, I have a shiny yellow one with red polka dots. Its branches are thinner, about 3-4 mm diameter, and smaller polyps that are white, which tells me that they contain no zooxanthellae. Is this true? Could the algae have died off? This coral is three months old in my tank and is doing very well. It's a litle more brittle than the purple. Any ideas what it is?

Thirdly, I have a blood red one with white polyps. Its branches are tighter together than the first two, and I find it's a bit more temperamental. It opens fully for 3-4 days, then closes for a week or two. Water conditions do not change in this period. I moved it to a darker end of my tank because diatoms were settling on it. It is situated right beside the outflow of my protein skimmer. It does slough off a kind of cellophane type skin when it opens up, so I've been trying to blast it with a baster, but it's still a bit pissy. Can you put a name to it? I understand that my descriptions are a little vague. The retailer I bought them from is having problems with them opening up, and with them being attacked by hair algae.

(Don't mind the stationery, I'm in the pub writing this!)

It took about a month for the polka-dot to open up fully, but now it's in full bloom, all day and all night. I've transplanted a cutting from a section that was being attacked by hair algae. This cutting is very healthy now, as is the parent colony. (thank you to the AquaStik people).

I've noticed a couple of times that the purple polyps fatten up and the tentacles form a flat disk stance. The next day my skimmer cup is full of pink slime. Could this be eggs? Also, the polka-dot emits a milky white stream out of the polyps on a lower long branch. I've tried sucking it up and putting it under a microscope, but it dissipates too quickly and my microscope isn't powerful enough. Are these signs of good health? Or could this be the polyps emptying their stomachs?

I've figured that the purple species seems to be more abundant in lagoons on sandy bottoms in full light. The other two (it's bad to assume, but...) I would assume come from deeper, cooler water with less light.

Now in regards to breeding, I've read that species that live in lagoons tend to be either just male or female, and species on the outer reefs tend to be asexual. With that in mind, would it be possible that the polka-dot could (if I assume right, let's assume I'm right... feel free to cut me off here) self fertilize itself? That would explain why only one branch emitted this substance. Also, could a one-sex colony change its sex if removed from the parent colony?

I feel I'm asking too much and haven't begun asking. The tank itself is 35 gallons, has an eggcrate plenum and at least a four inch substrate. There is about fifty lbs. of live rock. A corner overflow box with an aquaclear powerhead pumps the spill into a five foot tall four inch diameter homemade counter current protein skimmer that empties back into the tank. Four forty-watt tubes (2 Actinic and 2 Hagen marine Glow) are all on timers, with a fouteen hour photoperiod. There are three 301 powerheads on timers for a quasi-surge effect.

All nitrogenous products are at zero. I cannot get a three inch piece of *Caulerpa racemosa* to grow much. If it sprouts shoots, leaves die off to replace it. The only hair algae I get is from newly introduced specimens, and it is soon eaten or dies off. I feel guilty that perhaps things are starving, although I do feed my tank. I feed my corals baby brine shrimp and a homemade concoction done in a mortar and pestle. It consists of 5 to 6 freeze-dried krill, 1 to 2 drops of halibut liver oil, and a tiny bit of powdered amino acids (this comes in capsules and lasts me about 1 and 1/2 months). I find this is good for growth, and I get good results. I use a piece of 2 foot rigid airline that perfectly attaches to an eight ml feeding syringe. This is fed approximately once every two days.

Other inhabitants include a mushroom anemone colony (in a quiet corner) that spits off babies every so often, an open brain coral that has come back beautifully after a nasty bout with a bi-color blenny (it took me too long to figure that one out), an umbrella *Sarcophyton*, a *Condylactis* anemone, a tigertail cucumber, a serpent star, a 14" red spiky brittle star, a few gazillion skinny brittle stars, a half dozen each of blue legged hermit crabs and *Turbo* Grazers, a breeding pair of *Lysmata amboinensis*, whose young I've tried six times to rear, only getting as far as 28 days, a belligerent Royal Gramma, an orange spotted goby and *Alpheus* sp. partner, and finally a newly introduced tridacnid clam. The reason for the clam was to a.) Beautify my tank some more and b.) help drop the calcium level in my tank. I noticed a 100 ppm drop in calcium in three days after its introduction. I double checked this and have never had that happen before. That's one happy clam!

Last question. How high is too high for calcium? It always ran at 500 to 550 ppm, and the day I introduced the clam it was 600 ppm! The lowest it has ever been was 450 ppm. I'm using Red Sea Fish pHarm's test kit. The only additives were SeaChem's Reef Complete (less than 1 ml per week) and Reef Plus (2 ml once a month).

For over one month I've used no additives, except for water changes. I use Kent Marine Mix for salt. The water I use is a combination of bottled distilled water and D.I. water from a tap water purifier. When I purchased the clam I also purchased some kalkwasser mix because I was told that clams grow fast and use a lot of calcium. I've yet to use it as I don't want the calcium level to shoot up. The alkalinity is always 3 meq/L or higher and pH is 8.2 to 8.4. Today the calcium was somewhere between 450 and 500 ppm, so it is dropping. Anyways, thanks. This letter is going to be mailed. The others I have written I've always found the answers for myself, so if you could, I'd appreciate it.

Sincerely, a very interested reader, Martyn Rogers, Ontario, Canada

P.S. Thank Joyce Wilkerson and Dana Riddle for me, if you can. They've helped me too.

A. Ok, I will. Thanks Joyce and Dana!

Mr. Rogers wrote this letter on the backs of 3 promotional placemats for the 1996 Guiness Bar Games. Based on the length of his letter and the uniform appearance of his handwriting I don't suppose he had much to drink, but his stream of conciousness style letter is a bit funny eh?

Most of the gorgonians you refer to are Holaxonians, as you guessed. Some are not. For example, your polka-dot gorgonian is *Diodogorgia nodulifera*, and it is a Scleraxonian, belonging to the family Anthothelidae. You noticed it was more brittle than the purple gorgonian. Good observation! That quality relates in part to the construction of the tissue which distinguishes it from Holaxonians, though some Holaxonians such as *Pterogorgia* spp. can also be brittle, for other reasons. *Diodogorgia* occurs in deep water in Florida, where most aquarium specimens of this species originate. It lives most frequently on hardbottoms with strong tidal currents, but also occurs under ledges or on deep walls. *Diodogorgia* is not photosynthetic, so it needs to be fed.

I can't tell what your purple gorgonian is since your description is too vague. It could be a *Eunicea* sp., though these are usually grey or brown, only occasionally really purple. The blood red one could be a red morph of *Diodogorgia*, but it could also be any of a wide variety of species, including ones from the Indo-Pacific. Again, your description is too vague.

The skin that the gorgonian sheds is a waxy film that prevents algae from gaining a foothold on the gorgonian's surface. I've never before heard it described as being like cellophane, but the description is nice. I like it. Leather corals (*Sarcophyton* spp., *Lobophytum* spp., and many *Sinularia* spp.) also shed a waxy film, as does the stony coral *Porites*.*

So do *Millepora* spp. (Fire Corals) and *Heliopora* (blue coral).

There is a very good and widely available reference book for identifying Caribbean gorgonians. It's called *Reef Coral Identification*, by Paul Humann. It originally became popular in the dive industry as part of "The Reef Set," but it has been gaining in popularity among aquarists, who also appreciate the wealth of information and excellent color photographs for reliable identification. The section on Caribbean gorgonians is particularly wonderful for aquarists who wish to study them.

Volume two of *The Reef Aquarium* will also contain, among many other things, an extensive section on the identification of gorgonians, including those from the Caribbean. Charles Delbeek and I expect to have this volume available in mid 1997. Another book, *The Modern Coral Reef Aquarium volume* 2, by Svein Fosså and Alf Nilsen will cover gorgonians too. It should be available by the end of 1997. This book is based on the German volume 4 in their series, and those of you who have seen it know it is simply spectacular.

Your observations of the spawning of these gorgonians are exceptional. I wish you could take photographs of these events! It would be nice to have your photos in a book. You had some fishy assumptions and descriptions of coral sexual characteristics. It is true that corals may have separate sexes and that some may be both sexes, but having male and female organs (ie. being a hermaphrodite) does not make the coral "asexual." Asexual reproduction refers to cloning processes, which don't involve the union of gametes. I don't know whether portions of a single colony may be a separate sex from the rest of the colony. Nor do I know whether sex change can occur in corals, though I know as a general rule it does not occur.

Regarding the calcium dropping 100 ppm in 3 days I am skeptical that the newly introduced tridacnid clam is responsible. Newly introdced clams usually need a little time to acclimate to the new environment and settle down before they begin to grow rapidly. In a 35 gallon tank 100 ppm is not a whole lot of calcium, but it is more than I would expect a clam to remove from the water in 3 days. Where'd it go? Well, based on your claim of 600 ppm and relatively high alkalinity, I suspect the excess calcium just precipitated as calcium carbonate. In one of my own tanks I have seen this happen. My 15 gallon tank evaporates nearly a gallon per day, and the replenished water is kalkwasser, dosed by a pump controlled by a level sensing switch.*

*Now I use a Vario peristaltic dosing pump connected to a simple appliance timer to dose the kalkwasser only at night. This stabilizes the pH at night because it counters the drop in pH caused by the buildup of respired CO_2.

This high evaporation rate on such a small volume of water produces calcium levels over 550 ppm on occasion. Periodically the calcium and alkalinity do drop suddenly, but they build up again within a few days. Growth by the thick mass of corals and clams in this small tank could also play a role in the fluctuation of calcium level, but 100 ppm in 3 days is more likely caused mostly by precipitation.

You asked what is too high a calcium level. I'm not sure what the answer to that question is, but the answer is connected with the alkalinity. Alkalinity is more important for the corals than the calcium level. With high alkalinity corals can still grow rapidly at even low calcium levels (ie below 350 ppm calcium). When the calcium is high but the alkalinity is low, the corals don't grow much. High calcium levels often occur with low alkalinity since calcium carbonate and magnesium carbonate precipitate at high pH when the calcium and magnesium levels are at or above saturation level in the water. Further additions of calcium or magnesium ions will maintain the calcium and magnesium levels at saturation but will continue to reduce the alkalinity unless one adds the complementary ions that make up the alkalinity.

You need not worry about kalkwasser making the calcium "shoot up." It will elevate calcium, but not quickly since it (calcium hydroxide) is not very soluble. It can elevate pH very quickly, so it must be dosed carefully.

What the Kalkwasser does is supply calcium ions and hydroxide ions. The hydroxide ions react with organic acids in the water and therefore tend to prevent them from depleting the buffer capacity (alkalinity) of the water. The hydroxide ions also are the reason kalkwasser elevates pH. At the elevated pH the supply of calcium ions should cause a precipitation of some calcium carbonate, which would tend to lower the alkalinity. Often this does occur, but just as often it does not occur, and the alkalinity rises instead. The process is not completely understood and many experts enjoy arguing about it. I am not an expert chemist, but my understanding of it is based on a model I've accepted wherein the availability of CO_2 during the day is the determining factor for whether alkalinity is lost or gained. When CO_2 is not available during the day because plants are removing it from the water for photosynthesis, the plants will also directly lower the alkalinity by utilizing the carbonate and bicarbonate ions as a source of CO_2. If CO_2 is supplied by the respiration of animals or by artificial CO_2 injection, the excess CO_2 supplied can pair with the excess calcium ions supplied by the kalkwasser (remember that the hydroxide ions supplied by the kalkwasser are lost to neutralization reactions with acids produced by biological processes). Therefore the excess CO_2 can produce an increase in alkalinity when calcium ions are supplied simultaneously, at least in the model by which I understand the process it seems it can.*

I still agree with this model in principle. That is why I use a dosing pump connected to a simple appliance timer to dose the kalkwasser only at night. This takes advantage of the respired CO_2 that accumulates in the water at night when there is no photosynthesis to use it up.

Whether this model is correct or not, the fact remains that alkalinity can rise (as an indirect result) with kalkwasser addition alone, without buffers, when CO_2 is not in short supply (during the day), and the alkalinity can fall when CO_2 is in short supply during the day. The whole matter gets really complicated when one considers the effect of high pH on magnesium solubility, and the effect that loss of magnesum has on the buffer system. For a deeper review of this subject please see Craig Bingman's column, "The Biochemistry of The Reef Aquarium" in *Aquarium Frontiers* vol.3 no. 1. If it sounds like I keep recommending Craig's column, well it's because it is full of the most interesting topics.

September 1996

Q. Dear Julian,

Help! Strange deaths are occurring in Tanktown. Murder is suspected. The tridacnid victims were mauled in their sleep and couldn't give a description. Mrs. Maxima gold was the first. She looked so big, healthy, and beautiful until one morning... She was fully extended as usual but she had a spot that looked pinched or burned. A day or two later she started gaping and died.

A month or two later Mr. Crocea Blue, a resident of over 2 years, seemed to be holding his mantle funny, as if annoyed. Upon close inspection he had a pinched spot.

At the time of both injuries we performed stakeouts - day and night. We suspected the Pyramidellid brothers or, at first, a sweeper from Mr. Maxima's neighbor Caulastrea. The only suspicious characters spotted were a gang of amphipods. They were hanging out under the mantle and would flee into the body of the clams. When we removed the barely alive clams all we found was amphipods but we hoped we had removed the problem and the other clams would be safe.

Now two months later... big fat cousin Crocea Ultra is dying. First two pinch spots but he is still extended nicely. Today not so nicely. Yesterday Sister Squamosa showed a pinched area and today so does Uncle Crocea Blue. Sister Squamosa doesn't look too bad yet. She lives next door to an unaffected crocea on Bivalve Ave. Cousin Crocea Ultra and Uncle Crocea Blue live on the opposite side of town, a few blocks apart, on Mollusk Blvd.

In the beginning we brought the fish in for questioning. None had priors. The Yellow Tang moved in after the first two deaths, The other Tanktown fish are a Yellowhead Sleeper Goby and Two Convict Worm Gobies. All are upstanding citizens who volunteer for neighborhood clean up. The rest of the clean up committee consists of brittle stars, Turbo snails, tiny hermit crabs, and cucumbers. The other residents keep to themselves and seem obsessed with their looks. This includes lots of mushrooms, star polyps, *Porites*, *Ricordea*, green sea mat, and pulsating *Xenia*, also a *Caulastrea* sp., *Dendronephthya* sp., *Trachyphyllia geofroyi* a gorgonian, *Blastomussa wellsi*, *Turbinaria patula*, and a *Favia* sp., (with no sweepers yet).

Tanktown is a 30 gallon with corner overflow, sump, protein skimmer, live sand, VHO Fluorescents - 2- 36 inch Actinic and 2- 36 inch Daylight (on 7 hours), plus 2- 9 watt PL lamps (12 hours) used for wakeup and shutdown. Everything tests normal. Ammonia = 0, Nitrate =), Phosphate > 0.05 ppm, Alkalinity + 8DKH, Calcium = 400 ppm. We do our best to control the pH with Kalkwasser and CO_2 (via a homemade concoction of H_2O, yeast and sugar). However, the pH has been known to fluctuate as low as 8.1 and as high as 8.6. We add trace elements twice a week.

Well I've got to stock up on doughnuts. We have another stakeout tonight. Last night we observed the Amphipods crawling in and on the affected clams. Could they be the cause?

Juli and Brent Zapata, Tallahassee, FL

A. Oh all right everybody it was a cute letter, but the question was serious. No, the amphipods are not the murderers here. They merely live on the clams shell, feeding on algae and detritus mostly, but also on clam mucus. Whatever is bothering your clams is likely to enhance the mucus secretions by the clams, and this attracts more amphipods from the surrounding rock. You should also notice that your otherwise harmless brittle stars and tiny hermit crabs also become interested in the affected clams. In a previous Reef Notes column I described how stressed clams usually emit a distinctive pungent odor that has the unfortunate effect of attracting predators when the clams are most vulnerable to their attack. It is possible that whatever is bothering your clams is making them get stinky that way and then the attracted creatures (amphipods, brittle stars, hermit crabs, and bristle worms) are having a go at it and taking a few bites, which would kill the clams.

You'll notice that I have not specifically addressed the symptom of the "pinched or burned mantle." That is a seemingly distinctive symptom, but it does not tell me a lot. Was the "pinch" at the edge of the mantle or in the middle somewhere? I suspect what you mean is that a portion of the mantle was pulled in from the edge of the shell and folded. That symptom would have me looking for a stinging neighbor or pestering fish first, as you already did. If neither is present, as it seems from your description, I would remove the clam from the aquarium for observation. In general, when a clam appears ill it is a good idea to remove it (carefully!) and place it in another aquarium with strong lighting.

The symptoms you describe can also be observed when Pyramidellid snails attack, but since you say you haven't found them, I have to trust your observation. The snails suck "juices" from the mantle right at the lip of the shell, which can cause the "pinching" look. These snails are really very tiny, so please look closely!

I have seen another malady that kills clams and produces symptoms like you described. For a while it was common in wild-caught *T. maxima* imported from the Red Sea. The cause is unknown, but it appears to be a protozoan parasite, perhaps in combination with bacteria and other opportunistic organisms. A 1 minute freshwater bath for still vigorous clams seems to help, but if the clam is placed back into the same tank, it becomes re-infected. Treatment with Streptomycin (5 to 7 ppm) also may help, as the cause of death is often bacterial infections that overcome the already stressed clams. Such treatment must be done in a separate aquarium from the display.

In our book *The Reef Aquarium* vol. One, Charles Delbeek and I discussed the numerous maladies and parasites commonly affecting giant clams. A very comprehensive new book called *Giant Clams* by Daniel Knop provides an even more detailed discussion of diseases, including some new ones. This book, which also covers all aspects of clam biology, reef aquariums, aquaculture, lighting and system techniques should be available from your dealer by the time this column is printed.

The study of giant clam biology began only quite recently, so we have much to learn. Based on my own experience the symptoms you described could be parasitic snails, a boring polychaete worm (as shown in *The Reef Aquarium*), or a microorganism. If it is protozoans, I have no definitive cure to recommend, only a freshwater dip followed by observation in a separate aquarium, perhaps with antibiotics as I just described.

Q. Dear Mr. Dewey, I write to ask advice on the best method of attaching stony corals and soft corals to living base rock in a reef aquarium.

My tank is five feet by two feet six inches by two feet, well stocked in corals containing several species which are precariously perched (in the main). To my regret (and that of the corals), they regularly roll off onto their tank mates, get stung and damaged in the process. This recent development came about from receiving several corals from a friend. Sadly, space does not permit improved positions for each piece and the nightly march of abalones, urchins, starfish, and other creatures does not help.

An advertisement appearing in November '95 FAMA magazine (page 43), "AquaStik - Epoxy putty for underwater use" reads glowingly of the product and its properties. It seems "the answer to my prayers." However, here in Perth, Western Australia, Aquarium Stores and all those that I and friends know of (in the trade) have no experience or knowledge of this product let alone stock it. This raises many questions in my mind that could best be summed up by: What are your thoughts and experiences? Is there any risk to the tank specimens? Availability and price? Are there alternatives, better methods of achieving the same result?

Kind Regards, Frank Krause, Perth, Australia

A. Don passed your question along to me, which affords me the opportunity to comment about a product that I helped develop, which my company sells. I will do my best to avoid making a response that ends up sounding like a sales pitch, and those of you out there who are rolling your eyes about that, please be patient. I will give as objective an answer as I can.

In *The Reef Aquarium volume* one Charles Delbeek and I discuss the use of underwater epoxies, which we learned about from Bruce Carlson and Ken Yates, Tom Frakes, and Joe Yaiullo. We saw that this kind of material could be used safely and that the resulting stability it afforded greatly enhanced both the survival of the corals and the aesthetic appeal of the aquascape.

Merrill Cohen of Aquarium Products, Inc. urged me to consider bringing to market an epoxy like the ones discussed in our book. I experimented with different types with the thought of developing an affordable, easy to use product for the aquarium industry, and of course it had to be non-toxic to marinelife. I also wanted the material to be inconspicuous when used in a reef aquarium. The result was AquaStik, which matches coralline algae when mixed, and which comes in the convenient 2 ounce two-part stick epoxy format, which is the simplest to use.

Advanced hobbyists were trying the different epoxies Charles and I had recommended in our book, and I was discouraged by the thought that AquaStik might not be able to compete, since it is more expensive than some of them. I have to thank Jim and Cathy Duncan for convincing me to bring the product to market.

Aquarium Systems, Inc. recently introduced another two-part stick format underwater epoxy called HoldFast, which comes in a 4 ounce stick that is aqua-green before mixing but white when mixed. The price is very competitive and the product works very well too. So now there are even more choices! In addition, at the time of writing this article my company is also introducing a 4 ounce stick that is competitively priced. It is grey when mixed, and it is called AquaStik Stone Grey. We developed this product to have a neutral color in all situations, including freshwater aquariums.

To answer your specific questions, my experience with these epoxies has been very good, though as I'll explain in a moment they do require a bit of practice and understanding to use properly. There is no risk to tank specimens. I have seen no harm done to the fish, plants, or invertebrates. Regarding availability, I know you can get these epoxies now from your dealer in Australia. They are also readily available here in the USA and in Europe. The price varies at the retail level, but you'll find they are not expensive at all, especially compared to the loss or damage to corals from falling.

There are some things that need mentioning regarding the use of underwater epoxies. First of all, although they are not toxic to marinelife, they do initially leach organic compounds into the water while curing. Once cured (after 24 hours) they do not leach anything into the water. The substances leached into the water are harmless, but they do tend to make a protein skimmer foam more than usual. For that reason I recommend turning the protein skimmer off or reducing the air input to the skimmer for 24 to 36 hours after using the epoxy.

As I said, proper use of underwater epoxy requires understanding, practice, and of course patience and planning too. Underwater epoxies are NOT superglues! Many aquarists have the impression that the epoxy will bond on contact and hold a heavy object in place, but these epoxies do not work that way. They work more like concrete than superglue, though the consistency of the stick format types is like clay or putty.

The thick (as opposed to runny) consistency of the stick format epoxies makes them the perfect solution for attaching gorgonians. Simply find a hole to insert the gorgonian base or stem in, and then push epoxy into the hole and around the stem to secure it in place.

This exercise demonstrates the best use of underwater epoxy: to surround a stem or peg, like concrete does around iron rebar. Therefore, to create a natural projecting position for a large piece of coral, one should first insert a wooden or plastic rod into the base of the coral to make a peg. Insert this peg into a hole in the rockwork, using epoxy between the coral and rock to cement the piece in place. For small coral fragments one can surround the base with epoxy and push the blob and coral fragment onto a rock.

Attaching corals to glass with epoxy requires some experience and skill. Two main obstacles are getting a good bond with the glass, which requires that the glass is clean and that some pressure be applied to squeeze out the water from between the epoxy and the glass, and supporting the weight of the piece until the epoxy cures. There are two methods that have worked well for me. One involves the use of a set of the magnets used to clean algae off the aquarium panes. The other method uses styrofoam as a float. In either case the glass must first be cleaned with a razor blade to remove all algae or other encrusting growth. If the styrofoam float method is used, one makes a harness from rubberbands and/or string to tie a block(s) of styrofoam to the coral so that the coral is suspended at the proper height and angle to simply push it into place where it will be attached to the glass. Once the bond is made and the epoxy is cured (after 24 hours) the harness assembly can be cut and removed. The magnet method works for slender pieces placed flat against the glass. Basically a magnet outside the aquarium supports the position of a magnet inside the aquarium, placed below the piece being bonded. The magnet supports the weight of the piece until the epoxy cures. In either case, a sufficient quantity of epoxy is placed as a ball or cone in the center of the piece so that when pressure is applied the spread epoxy will cover most of the base and still be about 1/4 to 1/8 inch thick. The pressure must be applied evenly (by hand usually) for about two minutes, which can seem like an excruciatingly long time if the position is an awkward one.

Suspending pieces of coral or rock from the glass affords a very natural look and opens up some really creative possibilities for aquascaping. However, there are limits to the size and weight of pieces that can safely be attached to the glass. One should not attempt to attach dense pieces larger than a fist. Fragments of coral attached to the glass by epoxy will grow and form further attachment with the glass, supporting their own weight as they grow. In this way it is possible to have an aquascape growing from the walls of the aquarium suspended over the sand bottom. Fish that live in caves can swim in their natural upsidedown position and non-photosynthetic corals that live on the undersides of ledges can be attached naturally there with epoxy.

Underwater epoxy is also useful to help solidify the structure of the reef made of live rock. If the rocks are fitted together with plastic rods or with cable ties, epoxy can be used in between at points of contact to give more rigidity to the structure. Underwater epoxy does not have the ability to support very heavy pieces, but it can form joints between pieces, tending to prevent movement.

There are some other uses for underwater epoxy. Peter Wilkens told me he uses AquaStik to kill *Aiptasia* anemones. He simply smothers them with it by pushing some into the crevace into which the anemones retract. Some aquarists have used underwater epoxy to halt the progression of protozoan infections (something akin to white-band disease) in small polyped stony corals. The brown jelly-like infected tissue is siphoned off and the epoxy is placed like a bandaid over the bare skeleton and up over a small portion (about 1/2 inch) of the live healthy tissue. The technique apparently smothers the protozoans and the coral tissue grows back down over the epoxy. Finally, underwater epoxy can be used to repair leaky plumbing. For really bad leaks or cracked pipes it can be used as an emergency temporary repair, but the part should be replaced as soon as possible. Small leaks can be permanently repaired by pressing epoxy into the leaking joint. Epoxy should not be used for gluing glass together or for repairing leaky tanks. It does not have the elasticity of silicone, nor does it stick to silicone.

I've already mentioned that there are a few types of epoxy to choose from, but you asked if there were alternatives to underwater epoxy. There are, but each has its limitations. For attaching coral pieces underwater right in the tank there is simply no beating underwater epoxies. If you have the ability to make the attachment outside the aquarium, then there are some other options, such as cyanoacrylate glue, hot melt glue, and quick setting cements.

As described in *The Reef Aquarium* Vol. One, cyanoacrylate glues are very useful for attaching small coral fragments to rock. They can be used underwater, but work best when the surfaces being bonded can be at least partially dried. The drawback to cyanoacrylate is that the bond does not have much elasticity, so it will sheer and separate if it is agitated or jarred strongly before the coral has had time to grow new tissue down over the rock. The beauty of cyanoacrylate glue is that it allows one to spot glue tiny bits of soft tissue, which is most useful for aquaculture of soft corals and anemones. LeRoy Headlee of Geothermal Aquaculture Research Foundation in Boise Idaho told me about his experiences with using cyanoacrylate for attaching *Xenia* and other soft corals. I had never used it for that purpose, and was really impressed when I tried it. LeRoy has prepared an article about using cyanoacrylate in aquaculture for *SeaScope*, which should be available by the time this column is printed.

Hot Melt Glue is another alternative for attaching corals to rock outside of the aquarium. It works well for small coral fragments and has better elasticity than cyanoacrylate. It can also be used for attaching larger corals to rocks, but as with underwater epoxy, it is best to incorporate plastic or wooden rods to help provide a more structural attachment to the rock.

Quick setting cements such as Thorite were also mentioned in *The Reef Aquarium* and in a recent *SeaScope* article. These cements are most useful for building strong structures with limestone or live rock. Quick setting cement can support heavy pieces, unlike epoxy. However, while the epoxy can be used in an established aquarium, the quick setting cements are best used when the aquarium is first set up, during the construction of the aquascape, as they are best applied to a dry or semi-dry surface. They can be used of course for attaching a piece of coral to a rock outside of the aquarium, which can be placed in the aquarium after the cement has cured. A temporarily lowered water level could also be employed.

Happy Sticking!

October 1996

Q. Hi Julian,
You don't know me, I'm just another aquarist writing to tell you how much you are appreciated for what you do for us. Of course I have questions that I would like to pose to you in hopes of some answers regarding my reef tank. The first I can think of is regarding some *Ricordea*. I purchased it last summer in Ft. Lauderdale from "Jack" at Reef Life Inc. Is there *Ricordea* that can do well in low light? I've tried high intensity light and the *Ricordea* shrivels up against the rock and looks like it's really getting hurt. I would get the impression that it was getting burned. I called Jack and he said to

lower it in my tank. You know the statement if it works don't fix it well, I have a piece of *Ricordea* in a quarantine tank (yes I use one!) and it looks great! It only gets a 15 watt. Bottom line- What happens to *Ricordea* if it gets low light or too much light?

What are the nutritional needs of the Diamond Back Goby? Amphipods are in my tank but I don't believe the goby gets enough food so I take frozen foods and stick them into the sand about once a week or so. He eats it up no problems.

Barry Ardolf, Brooklyn Park, MN

A. Many corallimorpharia prefer indirect light, and *Ricordea* is no exception, though it does occur at times in places where it receives fairly strong illumination. *Ricordea* grows on hard substrate, usually on the sides of old coral heads, so that it is oriented perpendicular to the water surface. This orientation reduces the light intensity, even in shallow water. In deeper water *Ricordea* can be found growing over horizontal substrates. I have seen *Ricordea* occasionally in shallow water on a horizontal substrate, and in this situation it is typical for it to be very pale brown or slightly bleached... pale yellow in color. On occasion I have seen the wonderful pink and orange varieties in shallow water with strong illumination, and I am certain that these color varieties of *Ricordea* can take (and appreciate) bright light.

However, there is a difference between bright light in nature and bright light in our aquaria. In nature the bright light can be much brighter than in our aquaria, but more importantly it also differs by not being constant. The passage of clouds and the angle of the sun cause the light to vary in intensity. The passage of clouds in particular provides frequent brief periods of rest from the intense light. In our aquaria the light sources do not provide these rest periods. Strong illumination, particularly if it has a high quantity of UV wavelengths, stimulates the production (via photosynthesis by zooxanthellae) of toxic high levels of oxygen in the tissues of the host anemone, corallimorpharian, or coral. I should clarify that the molecular oxygen produced is not so problematic. When the anemone is illuminated by high intensity light, the energetic UV wavelengths in the presence of photosensitizing agents such as chlorophyll and flavins act synergistically to produce singlet oxygen and the superoxide radical (O_2^-), which is very reactive and readily forms hydrogen peroxide H_2O_2 (Shick, 1991). If you've ever poured hydrogen peroxide on a cut or put it in your hair you know it is also very reactive, and not something you want accumulating in your tissues! It should be no wonder why the *Ricordea* shrunk up and looked burned to you. I had discussed this problem in "Reef Notes" many years ago and didn't know at the time what was causing it. For a while there was this mysterious ailment called "burning" that I and others attributed to metal halide lights. As I pointed out in subsequent columns and in the book *Reef Notes Revisited and Revised* 1, I was wrong about attributing the problem to the lights. It was true the light had something to do with it, but there was nothing inherently wrong with the light itself. This was an effect of superoxide production, and the problem can be solved through shading or through the addition of trace elements, as I'll mention again in a moment.

Dykens and Shick (1982) describe the enzymatic defenses utilized to counter the effects of the superoxide. In one strategy the enzyme superoxide dismutase keeps cellular levels of superoxide low while other enzymes, catalase and peroxidase, convert the hydrogen peroxide produced into water and oxygen. Other biochemical antioxidants may also be used instead of enzymes (Tapley, Shick and Smith, 1988). Dykens (1984) showed that zooxanthellae have high levels of superoxide dismutase activity, and the enzyme used is a form with copper and zinc ions, a form not known from other unicellular eukaryotic algae.

What is mysterious is the effect of trace elements on this condition. Iodine (as potassium iodide) seems to help prevent this problem, and it is possible that other trace elements help also. Perhaps the trace quantities of copper and zinc from added weekly supplements assist in the formation of the zooxanthellae's special enzymes. Perhaps there is an antioxidant effect achieved by the iodide being converted to iodate, as suggested by Buddemeier in Delbeek and Sprung (1994). With all the talk about antioxidants and health lately, it's no wonder this has application to the subject of reef corals, anemones, etc.

For most photosynthetic cnidarians adaptation to the artificial light is just a matter of time, and it involves changes in pigment density and quantity of zooxanthellae. For some the adaptation is difficult, and if they are daily stressed by light intensity that produces toxic oxygen radicals beyond their physiological capacity to detoxify them, they may never adapt. As I explained, trace elements do seem to help a lot, though the reasons are not thoroughly understood. I mentioned that the light in nature is pulsed because of the passage of clouds. The periods of rest provided do actually assist in preventing the accumulation of superoxide by limiting its production. It is not essential to duplicate this pulsing of the light, but it is possible to do it (Gutierrez,1991).

Let's see, I think you asked whether there were low light *Ricordea* vs. high light *Ricordea*. The answer is yes, sort of, but it needs elaboration. In my experience *Ricordea* requires a bit more light than the smooth disc anemones from the Indopacific. Under dim light *Ricordea* may initially expand large, but the polyps will become pale and gradually shrink. Under just sufficient light it will continue to grow, but slowly, and it may lose some of its color. Under ideal light, *Ricordea* retains its bright color and grows more rapidly, particularly if you feed the polyps... blackworms and mysis shrimp are readily accepted if the fish or serpent stars don't steal them. As you discovered, if the light is too intense the *Ricordea* will shrink, for the reasons I explained. If trace element additions do not make the *Ricordea* recover and adapt to the light, then it must be moved lower, and don't forget the orientation, which should at an angle or perpendicular, not horizontal.

You also asked about Diamond Back Gobies, by which I am presuming you mean *Valenciennea puellaris*. These are terrific bottom sifters a.k.a. "bioturbation organisms." The trouble with them, as you noted, is a tendency to jump and, that being prevented, a tendency to starve to death. The starvation is not a result of lack of appetite, as they generally eat well. Your technique of placing food in the sand for them is unique and, providing you don't bury too much there and foul your tank, it sounds like you may have developed a good husbandry technique. You may wish to feed yours more often, however, to keep it healthy.

Q. I've found these "things" in my 55 gallon semi-reef tank and I'm not sure if they are copepods or mantis shrimps. I know it sounds strange to confuse the two, but I've talked to at least ten people on this and we're split on what they are. My tank is a 55 gallon with only 15 to 20 lbs of live Fiji rock. There are also a few fish, cleaner shrimps, Astraea snails, etc. The tank has been set up since April.

About two months after adding the live rock I started seeing these "bugs." As the bugs grew they started to look amazingly like mantis shrimps. Currently there are at least six of them in my tank, but there could be hundreds. They are from 1mm to 8mm long. After about 2mm the "praying mantis" arms are distinctive. So are the "swimmerets" in the tail. When spooked by the flashlight they curl their tail up under the body. It appears to be evenly segmented from tail to head. The "body area" appears to be segmented but inflexible. They are grayish brown. I think it has five pairs of legs not including the swimmerets and the praying mantis arms, but these guys don't sit still long enough for me to count.

From a physical description, we believe that they are mantis shrimps. However, because of their size, numbers, and the time of their arrival they seem more like copepods. Also, every book we've looked at says that mantis shrimps don't breed in captivity (and there aren't any parent shrimps, thank God).

So, the #1 question is: Should I worry?

The other questions are: If these are copepods, why haven't other aquarists seen these buggers? If they are mantis shrimps, then how did they survive/breed in my tank?

Thanks, David Kessner, Fremont, CA

A. Dear Dave, of course you should worry. You love to worry, don't you? Why accept that you only see six bugs in your tank when you can just imagine that there could be HUNDREDS? There must be hundreds! Based on your description, the bugs seem to become mantis shrimps right before your eyes. Your imagination is so powerful that you've obviously convinced some of your friends as well that these are mantis shrimp. Why stop there? Did you here about the giant mantis shrimp that crawled out of an aquarium in Japan and terrorized an entire city for two days until they brought Godzilla out of retirement to stop him? This was a big embarrassment for the aquarium industry there, and I understand that Godzilla lost an eye and two toes, and his agent (from Hollywood, CA) is suing. To put it mildly, this may just be the beginning.

Your creature feature sounds like run-o-the-mill amphipods to me, no worries. They eat algae and detritus, which makes them very desirable. Yes, it's true I've had letters like yours, sort of, before, and I've explained the benefits of amphipods a thousand times (or so it seems). However, just last month when an aquarist asked me if I thought amphipods might be irritating his giant clams I replied that I didn't think so. Well, I'd like to revise my comment a bit to say that generally amphipods are harmless algae eaters and detritivores, but SOMETIMES some species might get a taste for flesh, such as clam meat, particularly if there are very large numbers of amphipods. I almost hesitate to say it for fear that aquarists might go overboard and try mechanical means to eradicate amphipods, which they should not do! If there is a large number of amphipods in the tank, a mandarinfish or scooter blenny can get the populations down, as can many hawkfish, wrasses, or gobies. In general, however, proliferation of amphipods in the aquarium is a sign of good health. They are an important component in the natural control of algae and detritus.

Mantis shrimps simply don't occur abundantly, so I'm sure your guests are something else. There are other abundant small crustaceans that sort of look like mantis shrimps, but they stay small and eat detritus, just like amphipods do. Your description of the segmented head and the tail curling up have me reasonably confident that yours are amphipods. Did you look at the What Is That? section in *The Reef Aquarium?* It shows what amphipods, isopods, and copepods look like, so you don't have to lose sleep wondering if you have stomatopods.

References

Delbeek, J.C. and Sprung, J. 1994. *The Reef Aquarium. A Comprehensive Guide To The Identification and Care of Tropical Marine Invertebrates* Vol One. Ricordea Publishing Coconut Grove, FL. 560Pp.

Dykens, J.A. 1984. Enzymatic defenses against oxygen toxicity in marine cnidarians containing endosymbiotic algae. *Mar. Biol. Lett.*, 5: 291-301.

Dykens, J.A. and Shick, J.M. 1982. Oxygen production by endosymbiotic algae controls superoxide dismutase activity in their animal host. *Nature*, 297: 579-580.

Gutierrez, S. 1991. From a reef's point of view. *FAMA* 14(5):137-144.

Shick, J.M. 1991. A Functional Biology of Sea Anemones. Chapman & Hall, New York, NY. 395 Pp.

Tapley, D.W., Shick, J.M. and Smith, J.P.S., III.1988. Defense against oxidative stress in the sea anemones *Aiptasia pallida* and *Aiptasia pulchella. Amer. Zool.*, 28:105A (abstract).

November 1996

It has been a while since I have broken from the routine of questions and answers to open my big mouth and say something that gets people a little riled up.

In the near future in Reef Notes I intend to look into the role of the US Fish and Wildlife Service (USFWS) in the enforcement of CITES, the Convention on International Trade in Endangered Species, with respect to the importation of corals and other marinelife. At the moment I'm gathering information about the procedures that USFWS agents are supposed to follow.

As I write this (August of '96) I'm looking at an announcement I received by fax, which I will paraphrase here. The announcement states that the American Federation of Aviculture has been informed that the House of Representatives Committee on Natural Resources is presently planning a hearing on the activities of the Enforcement division of the USFWS sometime this Autumn, possibly as early as September. Although the hearing has not yet been formally announced, the focus is on the enforcement activities of special agents. It seems that there have been sufficient complaints registered with the Congress that they want to hear from the public about the type of treatment received at the hands of USFWS.

While most government workers in federal agencies are dedicated and responsible people who provide the country with good service in carrying out their duties, there are always a few people who go beyond rules and regulations in the pursuit of their own personal agendas. These few are a thorn in the side of the responsible agents, as well as a problem for the honest citizen. It is the activities of these agents that are of interest to the congress. This is an excellent opportunity for everyone who keeps and cares about corals, birds, or reptiles to exercise their democratic rights. If you have been harassed, entrapped, or experienced unprofessional conduct from USFWS agents you can bring this to the attention of your elected representatives. If you or anyone you know experienced a problem with agents in the Enforcement Division of the USFWS, please contact Kurt Christensen of the House Natural Resources Committee in Washington at 202-226-7338 (phone) or via fax at 202-225-6128.

I have personally been made aware of some experiences that marinelife importers have gone through that would make anyone's head spin or blood boil. For example, tridacnid clams and soft corals declared on the importation and CITES documents have been confiscated because they had small pieces of gravel attached, and USFWS agents considered this gravel scleractinia (stony coral) that should have been declared! In a more recent example I was called about a confiscation in which the import documents listed 15 *Scolymia*, a large round single polyp fleshy coral belonging to the family mussidae, while the agent believed the corals were *Cynarina*, which is another large round single polyp fleshy coral belonging to the family mussidae. In cases like this the importer orders corals based on an availability/price list supplied by the exporter overseas, and has no way to know whether the identification on this list is correct. In this *Scolymia* vs *Cynarina* dispute there is a further twist that I know, which makes the matter so much more interesting.

The "*Cynarina*" imported lately from Indonesia are actually a form in which the polyp does not match the typical form of *Cynarina lacrymalis*, the only officially recognized species in the genus *Cynarina*. In fact, I have shown pictures of this form to coral taxonomists and have been told that it is *Scolymia*. In my opinion, the collector/exporter made a good guess based on the appearance of the polyp, which was certainly expanded when he/she saw it. The living polyp looks like *Scolymia*, while the skeleton is closer to *Cynarina*. Charles Delbeek and I included this form in our book, *The Reef Aquarium* Volume One, on pages 418 and 419. Subsequently Charles and I had the chance to visit the Smithsonian and look at skeletons in their collection. We found skeletons of this mystery coral with tags identifying it as *Acanthophyllia deshayensiana*. To further complicate matters, that name was crossed out in pencil by a coral taxonomist named Hoeksema, who changed the name on the tag to *Cynarina*. Nevertheless, one could clearly distinguish these skeletons from the skeletons of *Cynarina lacrymalis*. So, at present THERE IS NO CORRECT NAME FOR THIS CORAL*. One could guess the name *Acanthophyllia deshayensiana*. is valid, or that it should be *Cynarina deshayensiana*, but that has not been formally published (though I'm writing about it here!)

*The world authority on coral taxonomy, Dr. Veron, adamantly believes these quite different forms belong to the same species, *Cynarina lacrymalis*. It is true that they differ both in the skeleton and the polyp, and that both forms can occur in the same region (this is the case in Indonesia and in the Red Sea), but there are also intermediate forms, which suggests either hybridization or, as Dr. Veron believes, that they fall within a spectrum of forms of this single species.

The point of all of this background information is that in this kind of situation it is clear that a MISTAKE has been committed, not a CRIME. No one was trying to smuggle in illegal animals. All the permits were obtained, paid for, and prepared with the greatest care possible. Unfortunately, these situations often end up with the animals in question being confiscated and placed by USFWS where they either perish or are not wanted, which is certainly not a very conservation oriented disposition. Furthermore, the importer is fined and declared a criminal, which permanently stains ones reputation, and the importer cannot see the confiscated corals to be able to educate himself and the exporter to prevent the mistake from happening again.

What I want to find out and report in this column is whether USFWS agents have the right to do this. It has been my understanding that the purpose of CITES (for animals on Appendix II) is to KEEP RECORDS of the trade in the species. With that goal it would seem that a mistake as in the above examples would not need "enforcement" action. It could be corrected simply by having the sharp-eyed agent change the documents (for the purpose of accuracy in reporting) when an error is observed. A small administrative fee for such a correction would be fair, and an explanation of the correction would encourage the importer to educate the exporter to avoid the mistake. This would be a pro business, pro conservation solution, and a useful service.

It is possible that there are enforcement issues and laws pertaining to the enforcement of CITES that I am not aware of, so I will visit this subject again once I have all of the regulations available to me. I encourage the readers who have experience with these situations to contact the above mentioned person in the House Natural Resources Committee in Washington.

Q. Dear Julian, I have a 55 gallon marine tank, which contains only fish and would like to add some live rock, *Caulerpa*, or possibly start a reef tank. But I'm concerned about the UV content of reef lighting. Most articles I have read say that reef lighting is safe, as long as you don't stare at the light. I know I can sit for hours in front of my tank and stare into it. I wanted to know if there would be any danger to the eyes and skin when observing my tank? If so, how much?

Also I wanted to know how much of a danger actinic, metal halide, and other reef lighting are? Are there any lights that are good for inverts and corals that do not emit UV light? Does a Vita-lite® bulb emit UV light? Could a Vita-lite® alone sustain a reef tank if the appropriate number of bulbs are used?

Sincerely, Steve Diamond, Brooklyn, NY

A. Another worry wart. I remember serious discussion about this back in the late eighties when Actinic 03 bulbs became popular and some hobbyists worried they might be harmful when in fact the bulbs do not emit any more UV than the full spectrum daylight and other full spectrum bulbs. Nevertheless you do have a point to be concerned, as I'll explain. First, however, you need not worry about looking at your tank for hours. The only harm that comes from this is being late for work, not finishing assignments, alienating your spouse (if he/she is not there watching with you), and letting the dishes and laundry pile up, among other things.

By the time it has passed through the water and the glass or acrylic window the light viewed by you through the windows of your aquarium does not have any UV wavelengths. However, if your light fixture is suspended over an open aquarium, and the fixture is above and shining directly on your eyes and face as well as the aquarium when you are there next to the tank watching, it is possible that you and your eyes and skin are exposed to some UV. In that case it is advisable to avoid having the light shining on your eyes and face for extended periods. You can accomplish that by having something to block the stray light whenever you are there watching the tank. Metal halide lamps and VHO fluorescents would provide the greatest quantity of UV light. In general, the quantity of harmful UV emitted is very slight for most types of lights used on aquariums, but some aquarists use fixtures with 400 or 1000 watt Metal halide bulbs, and these can emit a substantial amount of UV. Most of the harmful wavelengths are filtered out by the glass envelope surrounding the bulb in the screw-in type metal halide, while the glass or acrylic splash-guard lens of the fixture blocks out much of the remaining UV wavelengths. This lens is required for the HQI type lamps, which have no glass envelope.

You asked whether Vita-lite® bulbs emit UV. They do and were designed to do so. They were designed to provide a spectrum close to natural sunlight. Yes, you can sustain a reef tank with them alone if the appropriate number of bulbs is used.

Q. One of my customers asked me to ask you what are these things that look like sesame seeds all over his tank. They are on the live rock and glass, and are exactly the size and shape of sesame seeds.

Perry Tishgart, Champion Lighting

A. They are sesame seeds Perry. Your customer likes to eat a Big Mac while hanging over the aquarium, and he is obviously a very sloppy eater. Oh, ok fine, you want a serious answer. If you look around in the tank you will find one or more dark or checkered round snails. These are nerites, and the sesame seeds are their egg capsules. Nerites are beneficial herbivorous intertidal snails that feed on diatoms and other algal films. Although they are prolific egg layers, nerites seldom reproduce successfully in captivity. In nature the eggs are often laid in tidepools that are exposed to quite variable conditions, which may be critical to their development.

Q. I get a hard crust forming on the surface of the water in my sump. What is it?

Anonymous

A. I got this question by phone and forgot to write down the callers name. I explained to the caller that his observation was common for aquarists who drip kalkwasser into their sumps, particularly when there is very low water velocity in the sump. What happens is that since there is little water flow and therefore no opportunity for physical mixing, a thin layer of the kalkwasser "floats" on the surface of the sump over the denser saltwater below it. The pH in this kalkwasser is very high, which causes a precipitation of some of the calcium along with carbonate formed by CO_2 dissolving into the water right there at the surface where there is a high concentration of calcium ions from the dripping kalkwasser. The crust is calcium carbonate (limestone). The same crust can be seen in the container holding the kalkwasser.

To prevent this crust from forming in the sump the aquarist should administer the kalkwasser somewhere that has strong water flow. That way it will blend physically with the tank water. This reduces the pH before the calcium can precipitate with CO_2.

Aieegh!! I got a question about the use of underwater epoxy to attach *Helofungia actiniformis* (plate coral) to rocks. It is common for aquarists to attempt to position this coral on the rockwork only to be dismayed by the fact that the coral keeps tumbling down from its high perch. The reason may not be obvious to the aquarist unless he actually sees the piece fall... The coral tissue on the under surface of the coral swells with water and tips the coral over. For that reason Heliofungia should be placed on the bottom of the aquarium in strong light. In the natural environment they occur on sandy, muddy, or gravel substrates. They are free-living corals. Only small juveniles are attached to rock, and they break off after achieving a substantial size (big enough to survive on the soft substrates where they typically occur). Their ability to inflate the tissue with water prevents them from being buried in the sand or mud and it allows them to "walk" or turn themselves rightside-up when they get overturned. The underside of Heliofungia is covered with live tissue, so underwater epoxy doesn't stick to it. The coral should be placed on the bottom, not on the rocks. However, if the coral tissue has receded from part of the underside, it would be possible to use underwater epoxy to glue the piece onto rock. The same holds true for other fungiids such as *Fungia*, *Cycloseris*, *Herpolitha*, *Sandalolitha*, *Halomitra*, and *Polyphyllia*.

December 1996

Q. Could somebody tell me whether sea fans (gorgonians) need specialized lighting like corals do? Do they have any special lighting requirements at all? I haven't been able to find any information on this.

A. Several months ago there was a question in this column about gorgonians. I recommend that you read it (you probably have done so already). Yes, gorgonians do have special lighting requirements. Those that contain symbiotic algae (zooxanthellae) need light. Those which do not contain symbiotic algae do not need light. Some species which do not contain zooxanthellae also don't tolerate strong lighting, particularly if it has some UV wavelengths. There isn't enough space here in Reef Notes to show you every type of gorgonian and what it's requirements are. Most of them will be covered in *The Reef Aquarium* volume 2 when it comes out next year.

You specifically mentioned sea fans, a type of gorgonian in which the branches become fused in one plane to form a net-like blade. Most of the sea fan species imported for aquaria are not photosynthetic and are therefore difficult to maintain. There are three photosynthetic sea fans in the Caribbean that are easy to maintain in captivity, and they are quite beautiful too, in shades of purple or yellow. Unfortunately they are not legal to collect without a special permit in Florida and most other localities in the Caribbean, and commercial collection is not allowed anywhere, as far as I know.

All gorgonians (including sea fans) appreciate strong water motion, and they must be permanently attached to the rock, not just stuck behind the rocks like a background decoration. I have seen so many displays with gorgonians put behind the rocks where the tissue is dead except for the uppermost branches. I hope I can reduce this stupid practice of treating gorgonians like temporary floral decorations. To permanent- ly attach a gorgonian find a location where it will project out naturally into the current, and look for a hole in the rock into which the base can be inserted. If the base is too large to fit in the hole, trim it with a scissors. Use underwater epoxy to secure the branch in the hole. Photosynthetic species will grow new branches upward from a stalk oriented perpendic- ular to the light, a nice effect. The gorgonian can from the start be oriented upward in the way most are accustomed to growing. The beautiful photosynthetic "Purple Frilly" gorgon- ian from Florida is an exception. It is accustomed to growing from the sides of coral bommies and should be oriented accordingly, with the plane of growth perpendicular to the bottom of the aquarium.

Strong water motion will encourage the polyps to open. If the species is photosynthetic it does not need supplemental feeding (though it will trap some detritus, food particles, and will absorb dissolved nutrients). If the species is not photo- synthetic, it should be fed brine shrimp nauplii, Daphnia, copepods, pulverized flake food, clam juice, or phytplank- ton. These foods can be offered by pipette rather than filling the water with them, which would tend to pollute the tank. Stirring up detritus from the bottom provides additional food.

Some species shed a waxy skin once in a while, a process that helps them to clean their surface from attached algae. Just before shedding they will remain closed for a few days.

Strong water motion facilitates the process. Speaking of this process, I have another letter here (next question) asking about a leather coral, *Sarcophyton*, that seems to be closing a bit too often.

Q. Dear Mr. Julian I have a 220 litre reef tank, stocked with 35 kg of live rock. As equipment I have a Tunze 3115 protein skimmer, 2 powerheads, a heater and a chiller that keeps my tank temperature at 24-25 °C. As lighting I have been using 2 VHO bulbs (1 Actinic and 1 White, 95W each one) for 3 months, which made things better within my tank. In just one month the cyanobacters that used to cover my substrate have completely disappeared. I still have, however, some brown algae over the bottom and the front glass. Nevertheless, now it is more like dust, no more a hair algae like on page 269 of your book. I use carbon and phosphate remover continuously. I add CombiSan from time to time and I started using Reef Strontium from Seachem. one month ago which enhanced coralline algae growth. I also add kalkwasser every day with RO water.

I have had a golden crown leather for 3 months which follows the same routine: approximately 15 days opened and 5 to 7 days closed. The problem is that it has been closed for 13 days and it has developed a brown collar on the top of it (it is more like a "spotted brown"). I've noticed also that the first 4 cm of its body is darker than it used to be. Is this stuff brown algae? Is my coral endangered? What can I do to remove this stuff and how can I make my coral remain open more time? When it is closed it is not exactly attractive, don't you think? I can see that when the hermit crabs or my snails climb on it, it is really bothered. Sometimes my Coral beauty gives it a bite but I see no damage on the coral. I hope I can do something for the coral!

Miguel P. Galvao, Sao Paulo, Brasil

P.S. You have lots of fans here in Sao Paulo.

A. Glad to hear that. It is normal for leather corals to close up from time to time, as I mentioned earlier about gorgonians. Both shed a waxy "skin" that prevents attached algae from gaining too strong a foothold. When a leather coral remains closed chronically it is usually an indication that something about the water is bothering it, though it can also be disturbance from predators, irritation from algae, or from illumination that is too-strong. Strong illumination and predators are not the problem here as the leather coral would not open up at all if they were the problem. This kind of problem can be related to alkalinity, as leather corals are quite sensitive to changes in pH. Your figure of 8.3 for pH is excellent, but it does not tell me when you took the measurement nor the variance from day to night. Check the pH first thing in the morning before the lights come on. It will probably be well below 8.3. If the pH is really stable and high, your alkalinity is fine, and that is not the problem for your poor leather coral.

Another problem I've encountered personally and have heard reports about from other hobbyists is a negative reaction by leather corals to phosphate-absorbing media. I know that aquarists are bombarded with advice to control the phosphate level in a reef aquarium for best results, and that I too have emphasized the importance of controlling phosphate, but I have not promoted the use of phosphate absorbing media in reef aquariums. On the contrary, I strongly discourage the use of such media. For control of phosphate I recommend the daily use of kalkwasser and protein skimming, that is all. I have seen leather corals react like yours when various phosphate absorbing media (made from aluminum hydroxide) are used on the aquarium. I apologize to the manufacturers of such media for my harsh criticism, but in my opinion it is warranted. These media do work as claimed and they are certainly a way to control phosphate in fish tanks, but they can be harmful to some invertebrates, particularly leather corals, *Sarcophyton* spp.

Your coral beauty is merely eating algae off the surface of the leather coral. No harm done, as you suspected. I recommend that you continue your regimen, except that you should remove the phosphate absorbing media. You should make sure the leather coral is in a position where it receives a strong current intermittently, which will assist in in shedding the algae that has started to grow on it.

Regarding your disappearing cyanobacteria, this is a common occurrence, and aquarists like to believe that the disappearance is due to a particular light or some regimen when in fact those may only be factors in promoting the biological developments that make life difficult for cyanobacteria. Often if one does nothing at all they will subside once the environment becomes stable. The introduction to your aquarium of live sand from an established reef aquarium that does not have a problem with cyanobacteria (red slime algae) can provide a culture of the kinds of organisms that consume or outcompete the slime algae. In time these develop naturally, but adding a little culture is a great way to assist the process.

Q. Dear FAMA, I'm not sure whose department this would be for but I'll give it a shot. I was wondering if anybody knows if the Jaubert system would work with freshwater? I have a friend who has been very successful with it in his saltwater tank. I was wondering if it would work on my 135 gallon tank with Discus? Does anyone know if it is dependent on the chemistry of the salt water, or should it work with freshwater also? I was hoping you could tell me if it would be a waste of time to try it, or am I treading on some new ground (water)? Might I be on to something worth trying?

Dave Jepsen, Vancouver, Canada

A. That's a very good question, particularly for someone from Vancouver. (-- a joke, ok?). I had the same thought a few years ago, but with more elaborate theory, applying it to the creation of a freshwater planted aquarium. My thought was that the plenum should help conserve CO_2 in the system, as the breakdown of organic detritus in the bottom substrate by heterotrophic bacteria and the facultative anaerobes there produces CO_2 and generates some alkalinity as a bi-product. The use of a plenum which maintains a low oxygen level but not zero oxygen below the sand enhances the process. The exact effect on the chemistry will depend on the water's pH and hardness. Your main question I think was whether this system could be employed to control nitrate accumulation in freshwater. It definitely can. So it can be a complete biological filtration system for fresh or salt water.

I set up a couple of freshwater planted tanks using this method a couple of years ago and I am happy with the results, though I have not analyzed the water to determine if there is a tremendous benefit compared to systems using gravel but no plenum. The plants grow well for me without artificial addition of CO_2, but I can't say for sure whether the plenum is keeping any extra CO_2 available during the day. There is no nitrate accumulation, but that may be a product of the plant growth.

I suggest that you experiment with your idea and let us know what you find out, ok? Yes, you are "on to something worth trying."

Speaking of something worth trying, I wanted to congratulate T. Jay Froggatt who apparently is the first person in the USA to successfully rear *Pterapogon kauderni* (the Benggai Cardinalfish) in captivity. I have seen many reports of them carrying eggs, but his is the first confirmed hatching and successful rearing that I've heard about here. It occurred in August I believe, and was reported in "Fish Tales," the newsletter for the Desert Marine Society. I told Dr. Gerald Allen about it and he replied, "Bruno Conde of Nancy Aquarium wrote a couple of months ago to say they had a batch of young.

Apparently the incubation period was 28 days (long!) and the young left the protection of the parents immediately after hatching (contrary to my impression from field observations)." I guess it won't be long before we see tank raised specimens for sale, which is great news as this fish's natural range is very limited!"

January 1997

Last month I mentioned the successful rearing of *Pterapogon kauderni* by a member of the Desert Marine Aquarium Society. It seems reports are starting to come in from all over about rearing them. Also, sharp-eyed customers may notice that newly imported specimens sometimes are already carrying eggs or babies!

I talked about using Jaubert's system on freshwater plant tanks last month. This subject was also discussed in Aquarium Frontiers' vol. 3 no. 3. as well. Please refer to the Fishnet Q. & A. section there for additional comments about the idea.

More hopeful news about *Aiptasia!**

Recently there has been some excited discussion among advanced aquarists regarding a nudibranch, *Berghia verrucicornis*, that eats *Aiptasia* anemones. While other *Aiptasia*-eating nudibranchs have been reported (see *The Reef Aquarium* vol. 1.), this species is now being cultured so that in time it should be widely available as a biological control for this prolific reef-wrecking anemone. That is quite a breakthrough for the reef aquarium hobby!

Q. Dear Julian: I am fairly new to the reef tank world and need help! I have a 40 gallon tank with approximately 100 pounds of rock, five different corals, two anemones, feather dusters, five sea urchins, a small shrimp and 6 fish. I have a Gulf Stream Wet/Dry filter with a protein skimmer in the sump, a charcoal filter that hangs off the back of the tank and various pumps to move the water. Also, I have two 175 watt 5500K metal halide, one blue and one white actinic fluorescent.

My problem is the wet/dry. At least once a week it will get off balance in that it appears to be pumping out of the filter more rapidly than it is siphoning from the tank. The water level gets very low in the filter and too high in the tank. At times I can piddle with it and get it back into balance. At other times, nothing I do helps and I have to call the person who helps with my maintenance.

I've been told to use only two siphon tubes, then I've been told to bump it up to three, to keep the water level here, to keep it there. Adjust this lever, adjust that lever. Any of these suggestions will work for four or five days, but then I'm back to the hunt and peck system. The best news I've heard is that with the amount of live rock I have in the tank I could do without the wet/dry altogether. Even though this would mean purchasing a different protein skimmer, it would be heaven not to have to monkey around with this wet/dry.

Sincerely, Dianne Batson, Greenville, SC

*Eh, I'm not so convinced of the wonderful abilities of *Berghia*. In my experience they are difficult to culture and not effective at eliminating *Aiptasia* (though they definitely eat them). I prefer to use small specimens of the coral *Catalaphyllia jardinei* to sting *Aiptasia* and/or the shrimp *Lysmata wurdemani* to eat them.

A. Yes, of course you can run the aquarium without the wet/dry. You have plenty of rock for such a small aquarium! Please review old Reef Notes columns in the *Reef Notes* books and also see information about biological filtration in recent books about reef aquariums. Your experience is not very common, but it is a common potential problem with hang-on-the-back siphons. With hang-on-the-back siphons air trapped in the siphon tube(s), growth of algae in them, and changes in water density affect the rate at which the water drains down, as you noticed. Using an internal overflow drain instead (which requires drilling the tank) eliminates the problem unless: 1.) the drain size is too small (preventable right from the start); or 2.) the drain gets blocked by a clogged mechanical filter (preventable by not putting one there); or 3.) a large object goes over the falls and lodges in the drain hole (preventable by using a toothed screen at the overflow to keep wandering creatures in the aquarium). There is also the possibility of the toothed screen becoming blocked by algal growth or a wandering anemone, and this would also cause an over-filling of the aquarium.

Since I've advised you that you don't need the wet/dry, and since you have an established aquarium with no hole drilled in it, you have the option of running the aquarium without a sump. In order to do that you will need to keep the water level constant in the aquarium by means of a level switch.* The level switch turns on when the water level falls due to evaporation. It is connected with a pump (such as a submersible powerhead) that returns water to the tank from a remote freshwater reservoir. Many aquarists use this kind of arrangement for administering "kalkwasser," freshwater to which calcium hydroxide has been added.

*I prefer to use a peristaltic dosing pump instead of a level switch. In my experience the dosing pump is safer.

When locating the level switch inside the aquarium it is important to place it in such a way that snails or other crawling creatures can't get to it. If they crawl on it their weight could cause the switch to stay on, causing an overfilling of the aquarium.

I'm glad you realize the benefit of protein skimming. You could use internal protein skimmers, or a hang on the back skimmer, or pump water to a skimmer located beside or above the aquarium. Internal and hang on the back skimmers offer the simplest options since they don't require plumbing to install, but you must choose one(s) appropriately sized for the aquarium.

Q. Dear Sir, I am hoping that you or one of your associates could take a moment to answer a perplexing question. I am dealing with a "Dutch Aquarium System" wherin all invertebrates, corals, and fish are thriving, but I cannot get pink and purple coralline algae to thrive or proliferate. Would you be able to suggest a reason? The following parameters exist: Tank is 115 U.S. gallons with skimmer, steel wool, denitrator. Approximately 200 lbs. of live rock. Lighting: 2 x175 watt metal halide 5500K with supplemental actinic, 2 x 4 foot 40 watt fluorescents. The lights are 20 inches from the surface of the water. Calcium is 400 ppm, Nitrate 10 to 15 ppm, temp 77-78 °F, pH 8.3. Additives: Iodine and strontium. Kalkwasser is added to de-ionized water for make-up water. Accessories: U.V. sterilizer and a carbon filter cartridge. Also two powerheads to increase circulation.

Thank you in advance, Dennis Durie, Ontario, Canada

A. What you must do is to build a small shrine at the foot of your bed and make small daily sacrifices to the coralline algae gods. Ok, so you want the serious answer. You seem to have a pretty good system, but there are some vague and some strange things in your description. I have to assume that you meant polyester filter floss when you said steel wool. Tell me you haven't put steel wool in your tank, have you? You mention a "skimmer" but I'm not sure whether you mean a protein skimmer or just the surface skimming overflow.

I suggest that you remove the de-nitrator and rely instead on denitrification within the live rocks and sand substrate. You did not mention having any sand on the bottom. With the strong circulation you describe you could safely put an inch or two of coarse sand on the bottom. Please review old Reef Notes columns for descriptions of the use of live sand and the Jaubert System. If you want to incorporate a Jaubert type filter but do not want to tear apart the tank, the sand and plenum could be used in an attached sump. You should use a sand/gravel composed of calcium carbonate (aragonite).

Based on your good calcium level and pH, I am assuming your alkalinity is ok. Does the pH fall at night? Check it first thing in the morning to see how low it goes. If you add the kalkwasser with a dosing system at night when all the marinelife respires CO_2 you can prevent the pH from falling much, and give a boost to alkalinity. High alkalinity is an important stimulus to coralline algae growth. The precipitation of phosphate achieved with kalkwasser addition also helps promote coralline algae since phosphate impedes calcification.

You might try a "complete" trace element supplement that provides more elements than you are currently adding. Some aquarists note a correlation between the iron level and coraline algal growth, though this may be a result of other elements that are added to the aquarium in proportion with the iron via the complete supplements. The addition of iron must be done with caution as it can also stimulate undesirable filamentous algae if the conditions are right for algal growth: low pH = increased solubility of phosphate.

The lights you are using are fine, though you do have them raised up a bit too high... actually that should help to encourage coralline algal growth as coralline algae prefer to grow in shady, indirectly illuminated places. Normally I'd place the lights you are using only half as high as you currently have them.

If you really get the water moving (coralline algae like highly oxygenated fast moving water) and provide sufficient alkalinity and calcium along with proper illumination, it is only a matter of time before the coralline algae introduced to the aquarium with the live rock begin to spread. The addition of trace elements and strontium often encourages them to further proliferate. Beyond that patience helps, and one should not perform excessive water changes that disturb the environment.

On that subject...

Q. Dear Reef Notes, I have a 230 gallon reef tank that is up and running for fifteen months. There is a one-inch layer of large aragonite substrate and about two hundred pounds of

Fiji and Tonga live rock. When I established the tank I put the rock directly into the filled tank which is filtered by a very large venturi skimmer. Additionally there is a flow-rate of over 800 gph from the sump and another 800-1000 gph circulation from the wavemaker. Within two weeks all nutrient tests were zero except for nitrate which was at 40 ppm. I have an automatic water changer which exchanges new R.O./D.I. mixed saltwater overnight. At that time I set it to change ten gallons per night, figuring to accomplish an almost total water change in about a month. The nitrate slowly reduced to about 15-20 ppm, so I continued for a while with 3 gallons per day water change. After 14 months my nitrate was still about 10 to 12 ppm. I use only salts that advertise and test nitrate free. Two weeks ago I made three simultaneous changes: 1.) totally stopped water changes; 2.) added second 6500K 400 watt metal halide (the tank is now illuminated by reef type fluorescents for 12 hrs per day and two halides for 6 hrs, per day); 3.) instead of constant alternating of wave making I now pulse 35 seconds on and 25 seconds off (on at 1000 gph).

Guess what? My nitrate reading went straight down to zero! Why? I always thought that it if I didn't change water the nitrates would go up. I now am changing three gallons once or twice a week.

Ira Tommer, New York, NY

A. You made so many alterations at once that it is difficult to say what, beyond time, got your tank onto its current state of biological balance. When you have natural denitrification taking place in the sand and rocks nitrate does not accumulate, as you have finally discovered. Once you achieve this biological balance, as long as you use adequate protein skimming and keep up with trace element additions and the maintenance of calcium and alkalinity, the amount of water change required is really very little. When an aquarium is not so balanced periodic water changes make sense.

When the aquarium has a very strong capacity for denitrification the addition of food does not produce any accumulation of nitrate. The use of protein skimming further removes dissolved organic compounds and phosphate.

With this combination it becomes necessary to feed regularly. Many species of coral and tridacnid clams show signs of starvation otherwise.

The past month and a half has been rather fast paced and action packed for me. It started with a weekend in England courtesy of Underworld Products and the West Yorkshire Marine Aquarists Group (WYMAG). This marine conference featured lectures by Peter Wilkens, Jean Eckert of Aquarium Systems France, and me. We also had the opportunity to visit with U.K. super-aquarist David Saxby. Many thanks and congratulations to Dave Keeley and Des Ong of Underworld, plus Roy Meeke and everyone of WYMAG for their efforts in making this event the success that it was. Also special thanks to Dave Saxby for the VIP entrance at the Hard Rock Cafe, the great dinner, and the hand delivery of some new soft corals that I had seen at Tropical and Marine pet shop and in his aquarium.

After returning home to Miami, the following weekend I took off again to attend the H. H. Backer Trade Show in Chicago where Two Little Fishies (Daniel Ramirez and I) were exhibiting, along with special guest Alf Jacob Nilsen. Alf was in the country for MACNA, and at the Backer Show to promote his new book, *The Modern Coral Reef Aquarium* volume 1. The Chicago Show was very well attended and, compared to the other Backer show in Atlantic City, it was by far a more convenient location to exhibit. After the show I gave a lecture for the Chicagoland Marine Aquarium Society. Many thanks to Steve Messerges, Dennis Gallagher, John Brandt, and other club members who made the event work so well.

Alf Nilsen returned to Miami with Danny and me for a couple of days before we had to go up to Kansas City for MACNA, which was a blast, as always. This year's presentations were most interesting, from aquaristic as well as scientific points of view. Congratulations and thank you to Bob Hix and the Kansas City Marine Aquarium Society, along with MASNA staff and exhibiting manufacturers for making this such a great conference. Thanks also to Aquarium Systems, Inc. for sponsoring a special dinner for the speakers and organizers.

As if that wasn't enough, I just got back from Puerto Vallarta where I gave a lecture on captive husbandry of corals for the invertebrate session at the AAZV conference. So now I am home at last and here's another column.

Q. Hey Julian, Are you out there? Hello? No really, I wrote you about two months ago and never got an answer. That's ok because the problems I was talking about have become self limiting and my bristle worm problem is just about over thanks to one Coris wrasse!

I have just finished reading an article about "Natural Systems" and would like to try setting one up, but I would like your thoughts on the following:

Eng's natural system sounds great but it seems to me that it would have some problems.

1.) Won't air stones cause a foam on the water's surface?

2.) Can I use a powerhead instead or would this defeat the purpose since this system is based on a "nontraumatic" environment for planktonic life? 3.) What about water quality? Won't it turn yellow?

4.) Back in the 80's I recall how wet/dry filters became a "dead horse." I just finished reading an advertisement for "algae filters" which stated "protein skimmers damage your system!" Is this true? What are your thoughts on that statement? Is the skimmer the next dead horse on our way to the realization that the natural system is the only way to having a true living and complete reef?

5.) Did Eng use any calcium or trace element supplements?

6.) Did Eng do water changes? 7.) Did Eng use carbon? 8.) It also seems Eng's system relied on macroalgae for filtration. I have heard many times that macroalgae can release compounds in the water that are bad for corals. What are your thoughts on this?

Like I said Julian, I am very interested in any info on this method, so if you or anyone else out there can think of anything I left out please let me know. I would like to know if this system works better than the "Berlin" method I now use or if it's a waste of time setting up a tank based on a system others have tried and failed at.

Thanks, Tom Kaufmann, Old Monroe, MO

Q. Hey Tom, Gee, I wonder why I didn't answer your first letter... I'm glad to see that you have been inspired to try a simple natural system aquarium. I'll answer your numerous questions in order.

There was a similar question in my January 1993 column which generated quite some controversy in the editorial pages of *FAMA* because of my criticism of the algal turf filter. Please review that column (also found in Reef Notes, volume 3). Also see subsequent articles by me and Walter Adey in *Aquarium Frontiers* journal, and have a look at the suggested readings at the end of this column.

An airstone could cause foam on the water surface if the tank is heavily polluted or if an animal has died, but in general the use of an airstone actually helps keep the surface of the water clean. It serves a function something like protein skimming, though instead of the skimmed compounds being removed into a collection cup, they get deposited along the walls of the aquarium at the water line, and mixed into the water where they may be removed by activated carbon or decomposed by biological activity (bacteria, microorganisms). The main problem with the use of airstones is the formation of "salt creep." Salt creep is unsightly and also dangerous to the aquarium inhabitants since it can fall back into the aquarium and land on sessile invertebrates, causing tissue damage.

Using water pumps (powerheads) for water circulation is an alternative to airstones, but if there is no surface skimming and no airstone the water surface will quickly develop a film that impedes gas exchange and blocks light. If you have a surface skimming overflow, the surface film is removed from the tank and deposited in the sump. There it can be broken down biologically if no protein skimmer is used.

Regarding your concern about "plankton friendliness" of pumps, I don't consider this important at all, though many authors do. I don't think that Eng was particularly opposed to water pumps, though I never met him and therefore don't know for sure. He died in the 1980's. Svein Fosså, co-author of *The Modern Coral Reef Aquarium*, corresponded with Eng and is a good source of information about what Eng was doing. Dr. Cliff Emmons, author of numerous books published by TFH, also had some communications with Eng.

There has been some discussion in reef aquarium literature about creating a so-called "non-traumatic" environment for plankton (see for example Adey, 1991). My reason for not being concerned about plankton is that it cannot be cultured in significant density in a small aquarium with a stable diverse population of reef fauna that rapidly consumes it (i.e. the reef eats the plankton faster than pumps would destroy it and the biological stability of the microfauna in the rocks and sand prevents blooms from occurring). Furthermore, I have passed all sorts of zooplankton and phytoplankton through centrifugal pumps without causing any harm. A properly functioning protein skimmer, however, very effectively removes all sorts of plankton from the water, especially phytoplankton but also zooplankton, including larger organisms. I do not consider that a serious disadvantage at all, as I'll shortly explain, but I wanted to mention it because it is clearly demonstrable and contrasts with the completely harmless effect of erroneously maligned centrifugal pumps.

You asked if the water would turn yellow. Yes it sure will, but you can prevent the yellowing by using activated carbon.

Protein skimmers damaging the system? That is a most misleading claim. The next dead horse? Certainly not! The protein skimmer is the single most important filter device for maintaining water quality.

That protein skimmers can and do remove plankton from water is not damaging to water quality. It is damaging to plankton, sure, but not water quality. We are not trying to maintain plankton. We are trying to maintain a reef ecosystem. If we were trying to prevent destruction to plankton, then we had better remove all of the filter feeders too! I hope you can appreciate the truth in this.

To add a further twist, the fact that protein skimmers remove phytoplankton means they are a sort of algal filter... By exporting skimmed phytoplankton they do what is done when the aquarist harvests algae from an algal turf filter a.k.a. turf scrubber. In addition protein skimmers remove all sorts of organic compounds that otherwise accumulate or decompose, to the detriment of water quality.

Now this implies another question: what about successful systems that don't employ protein skimming? It certainly is possible to run an aquarium without a protein skimmer, as I have done quite successfully, but I can assure you that most systems are dramatically improved when a protein skimmer is added. When there is no skimmer, success is best achieved by relying on a thick sand substrate and live rock for complete biological filtration (nitrification and denitrification) that can effectively purify the water (the system employed by Eng and Jaubert). The main draw-back to these systems, one which is solved when protein skimming is used, is the lack of a means to export of phosphate. When air stones are used to circulate the water (as Eng and Jaubert recommend) some phosphate can be exported via aerosol. As I mentioned earlier in the answer, such aeration does achieve an effect approximating the protein skimmer, though it is not as effective of course. The addition of an algal turf filter is yet another means of exporting phosphate* and solving the problem, so you see it is true that a protein skimmer is not an absolute necessity. However, in my opinion protein skimming is by far the simplest to use and most effective means of water purification. When protein skimming is combined with the complete biological filtration found in living sand and rock substrates, one has a very good system for maintaining a reef ecosystem in closed aquariums.

*So is harvesting algae growing in the aquarium or in attached refugia.

You asked if Eng did water changes, or used any calcium or trace element supplements. From the articles he wrote one has the answer, sort of. No, he did not add prepared supplements for calcium or trace elements. However, he did use natural seawater, calcareous sand substrate, and certainly used unfiltered make-up water. Eng lived by the sea and could change water to replenish depleted trace elements and calcium, though he reported success without regular water changes (Eng, 1961). Presumably the unfiltered fresh-water he used to replenish evaporation supplied trace elements, and possibly calcium. Dissolution of the calcareous sand also supplied some calcium.

You asked if Eng used activated carbon. I doubt it. However, this does not mean that the water would not turn yellow in his system. It certainly would.

You mentioned Eng's system using macroalgae for filtration. In fact, what Eng did was to choose live rocks with red coralline algae and other red and brown seaweeds. The red seaweeds are slow growing and have a nice stabilizing effect on the decor and water quality. If Eng regularly added stones with red and brown seaweeds to his tank he was supplying a source of iodine and bromine, as the plants concentrate these trace elements from seawater.

Your question about macroalgae releasing compounds in the water that are bad for corals is based at least in part on my own speculation about it, which I wrote in this column a few years ago. In general, no, the algae are not poison-ing the water. However, when algae grow adjacent to corals they can kill them with noxious compounds, as can be seen in some cases when certain *Caulerpa* species send stolons across a coral colony, or when the cyanobacteria (blue-green alga) *Phormidium*, which causes "black band disease," settles on a coral. One thing that algae do that is not ideal for corals is that they compete for the same food. Algae in an algal filter consume the ammonia and carbon dioxide that corals (their zooxanthellae) need to grow. Not only do algae compete with corals for these inorganic nutrients, the algae also leach back organic forms of the nutrients, which may or may not be bothersome to the corals, which essentially do the same thing (Atkinson, Carlson, and Crow, 1995). Algae and coral communities both exhibit a net uptake of inorganic nutrients and a net release of organic nutrients (Atkinson, Carlson, and Crow, 1995), so dissolved organic nitrogen and dissolved organic phosphate may accumulate in closed systems that rely on algal filtration alone. By contrast, protein skimming produces water with low inorganic and low organic nutrient concentrations (Atkinson, Carlson, and Crow, 1995). There is much complexity to the water chemistry of closed systems with high diversity of species on a variety of substrates. The formation of particulate organic compounds and their use by living organisms in these ecosystems, for example, are processes that help to remove some of the substances leached to the water when protein skimming is not there to remove them directly.

Algae should not be considered detrimental. I have noticed that systems with a so called refugium attached (Adey, 1991) in which algae are cultivated in the absence of herbivory do develop nice diversity of microorganisms, and there is an overall positive effect on corals and other animals in the system. These refugia can be managed like algal filters too.

So, can you set up a simple system and grow corals? Absolutely. Without a protein skimmer? Certainly. Is it better to run a reef ecosystem full of corals and fish that way? No, a protein skimmer improves the system. Furthermore, when natural denitrification is actively proceeding in the substrate (gravel, sand, live rock) the presence of fish and/or addition of food is essential to encourage coral growth. The same observation could be made when algal filters are used: if the inorganic nitrogen (ammonia and nitrate) are effectively brought to very low levels, the corals may need supplemental food (directly or via feeding the fish) to really thrive. The addition of trace elements and maintenance of calcium are essential in systems containing large populations of actively growing corals. Lastly, the export of phosphate is critical to long term success, and protein skimming in combination with the use of kalkwasser (calcium hydroxide in the top off water) are highly effective at achieving this purpose. These are the shining attributes of the Berlin method. Natural systems are successful, simpler and less expensive to install, but their long term success can be improved with protein skimming, particularly when there are many fish in the aquarium.

Suggested Readings
Adey, W. H., Loveland, K. (1991) *Dynamic Aquaria*, Academic Press, New York, 640pp.

Atkinson, M.J., Carlson, B., and G.L. Crow. (1995). Coral growth in high-nutrient, low pH seawater: a case study of corals cultured at the Waikiki Aquarium, Honolulu, Hawaii. *Coral Reefs* 14:215-223.

Brandenburg, W. 1968. Filtration of marine aquaria. *Trop. Fish Hobby.* 17(4): 4-17.

Emmens, C.W. 1975. *The Marine Aquarium in Theory and Practice.* T.F.H. Publications, Neptune City, New Jersey.

------------ 1986. The natural system and the minireef. *Freshwater and Marine Aquarium* 9:71.

Eng, L.C. 1961. Nature's system of keeping marine fishes. *Tropical Fish Hobbyist* 9(6):23-30.

-------------- 1976. Stop killing the corals. *Marine Hobbyist News* 4(8):5.

Jaubert, J. and J.P. Gattuso, 1989. Changements de forme provoques par la lumiere, observes, en aquarium, chez coraux (Scleractiniaries a zooxanthelles). Deuxieme Congres International d'Aquariologie 1988 Monaco, 1989. *Bull. de l'Institut Oceanagraphique, Monaco,* No. special 5:195-204.

--------------, 1989 An Integrated nitrifying-denitrifying biological system capable of purifying seawater in a closed circuit system. In: Deuxieme Congres International d'Aquariologie (1988) Monaco. *Bulletin de l'Institut Oceanographique, Monaco,* No. special 5:101-106.

--------------, 1991. United States Patent number 4,995,980.

----------, Pecheux, J-F., Guschemann, N., and F. Doumenge. 1992. Productivity and calcification in a coral reef mesocosm. in *Proceedings of the 7th International Coral Reef Symposium,* in press.

Riseley, R.A. (1971). *Tropical Marine Aquaria: The Natural System.* Allen and Unwin, London.

Coral disease on the reef vs. the reef aquarium.

The past year or so I've noticed an increase in questions regarding sudden loss of small polyped stony corals to rapidly progressing diseases that cause the tissue to disintegrate. Some hobbyists observing this for the first time confuse the condition with "bleaching," which is just a loss of pigment or photosynthetic zooxanthellae, a less serious ailment. The rapid loss of tissue leaving behind white skeleton is not bleaching, it is death of the coral due to a pathogen. It is contageous and can sweep through and kill the corals in an aquarium in hours or days. Hobbyists discussing this condition in forums via the internet have been calling it rapid tissue necrosis or RTN.

In nature a condition of this sort called "white band disease" has been known for many years. More recently as scientists have become more aware of coral diseases, the white band condition has been subdivided into several distinct conditions. Although it is not yet proven, it seems apparent that the diseases affecting captive corals are the same as those in the wild.

One type of tissue necrosis that has been common in reef aquaria for years is caused by a protozoan, *Helicostoma*. It causes "brown jelly" infections in which the tissue is destroyed along a rapidly progressing front of gelatinous mass teeming with the protozoans, which consume zooxanthellae. It can affect small polyp stony corals, other stony corals, soft corals, zoanthids and corallimorpharia. It is a common cause of rapid death in *Euphyllia* species, and in this column several times I have described Dr. Bruce Carlson's one minute freshwater dip to halt the progress of the condition.

*See *The Reef Aquarium* Volume Two for a complete description of how to use this treatment.

Other forms of tissue necrosis have more mysterious causes. It is a general opinion (mine included) that most are caused by bacterial infections, but little is known about this. Dr. Craig Bingman (pers. comm.) recently halted the progress of a particularly virulent tissue necrosis event in one of his aquariums by administering a dose of Chloramphenical to the water.* This antibiotic, while difficult to obtain because of its recognized hazards to human health, is quite effective in the treatment of pathogenic bacteria that live in saltwater.

One type of RTN essentially is identical to the white band disease in nature. White skeleton is exposed along a front of rapidly disappearing coral tissue. In front of the skeleton the tissue appears healthy, behind it the tissue is gone. Another type affects whole branches at once, and ccauses the tissue to drip off the skeleton. Often the tissue appears perforated before it falls off. This latter condition usually spreads very rapidly, and may wipe all *Acropora* in the aquarium in a short period.

I wanted to offer for comparison some statements in a recent newspaper article about a tissue necrosis condition found near Key West Florida. The article appeared in The Key West Citizen, December 3, 1996, and was titled, "New killer attacks coral reef off Keys." The article describes a new type of tissue necrosis being called "White Pox" disease affecting elkhorn corals, *Acropora palmata*. The article states that the condition "has scientists and staff at the sactuary stumped. They have no idea what causes White Pox, how fast it spreads, how long it germinates and whether it is a bacteria, fungus or virus. The effects are clear: Tissue streams of the corals like mucus from a runny nose...(and it) causes tissue to melt off the skeleton in great globs."

This certainly mirrors the virulent RTN commonly afflicting *Acropora* species in captivity, and highlights the need for reef researchers to correspond with aquarists. We can help each other by filling in the gaps where we each are ignorant.

Interestingly, one of the regions where captive *Acropora* are imported from, the Solomon Islands, had a major die off of large *Acropora* colonies last summer when water temperatures stayed unusually high. It is common experience to see tissue necrosis suddenly appear within a few days after introducing a newly acquired piece of *Acropora*. Therefore the need to quarantine newly imported colonies is indicated.

Several months ago Mike Paletta suggested that the pathogen might be a virulent strain of the bacteria *Vibrio*. This remains a distinct possibility, and the effect of antibiotics (in the proper dosage) suggests such a bacterial cause. Unfortunately, it is unrealistic to attempt to eliminate such bacteria from aquaria...they are ubiquitous. Nevertheless treatment when an RTN event occurs can be effective. Dr. Bingman, Terry Siegel, Greg Cook, Robert Stark, Bruce Carlson, Charles Delbeek and others observing this condition are helping to elucidate the factors involved in its occurrence.

An important factor in the occurrence of this condition is the growth of established colonies such that the water flow in the aquarium is reduced by drag on the branches. Overshading by these branches also reduces light to the lower portions of the colony, which often are the first to get white-band type symptoms. When there is such reduced water flow and light, the condition spreads most rapidly. The presence of strong water flow seems to help prevent the spread of the disease.

From this we gather a few important tips: 1.) Keep the corals well pruned to prevent overshading and flow reduction and add more water flow if necessary; 2.) Quarantine new colonies 3.) Always break off several branches from a new as well as old colonies to establish them in as many aquariums as possible to minimize the potential of losing the species should any of the branches become affected.

When the disease occurs, my advice is to remove all affected colonies if possible. Healthy branches far away from the necrosis should be severed and maintained in aquaria separate from unhealthy branches. Underwater epoxy can be used as a band-aid at the progressing front of tissue necrosis, and this may halt the progression of the disease. Direct an even, increased water flow over affected colonies if they cannot be removed from the aquarium, but break and remove as many affected branches as possible.

Dr. Bingman will likely present his observations and suggestions regarding antibiotic treatments in future issues of *Aquarium Frontiers*. He and Terry Siegel have correctly recognized that this condition has serious implications for the reef keeping hobby as a whole: Aquarists who have invested a fortune acquiring rare and colorful *Acropora*, *Seriatopora, Pocillopora,* and other small polyped species risk losing everything, and this can easily result in many hobbyists getting out of the hobby. I can't stress enough how important it is to maintain these species in several aquariums to be able to re-establish species that can easily be lost in just one aquarium.

Q. Dear Julian

I am interested in trying some variations on the Jaubert substrate and wondered if you had any experience with any of these possible variations.

1.) I have set up a two-inch plenum with a four-inch aragonite substrate, with an underlying Sandpoint substrate heater designed for freshwater tanks. After several months of operation I turned on the substrate heater with rise in the aquarium temperature from 76° to 80° in the water above the plenum, but with associated dramatic improvement in the appearance of the tank in terms of decimation of nuisance algae and improvement of macroalgae (*Botryocladia, Caulerpa, Neomeris*, Mermaids cup). I would think a warmer substrate would be helpful but, of course, a chiller may also be required. Do you have any other observations on this approach?

2.) Instead of four inches of substrate with two inches of underlying plenum, it might be better to open the plenum to the water above the sand via plastic tubing, without or with airstones. The point is not to make an undergravel filter, but rather to double the surface area of the sand bed, with the previous "plenum" now fully oxygenated water. The void space would then be moved to the middle of the sand layer.

3.) Instead of a regular plenum, perhaps it would be better to break up the surface of the plenum and embed a series of small spheres in the substrate. This would allow the same volume of plenum, but a markedly increased surface area in contact with the sand, which may allow better diffusion of CO_2 into void spaces. Of course, alternatively, this could be done with regular pieces of very coarse aragonite sandwiched between two oxygenated layers.

4.) Denitrification requires an organic source of carbon. All the old denitrifying filters ran on some form of sugar or methanol. is anyone looking at diffusing an organic source of carbon below the sand bed? If you are going to experiment with this, what organic source of carbon would you use, and how much? What would happen if I infused glucose underneath the sand? Are there any deleterious effects of such an approach to watch for (other than the obvious production of hydrogen sulfide- I mean, could it stimulate blooms of algae or other unwanted biological effects)?

5.) Do we have any hard evidence that skimming affects the efficiency of the Jaubert filter? For example, do calcium levels drop when the skimmers are turned on, signifying less bacterial activity in the sand?

6.) Does anybody have any hard data yet about what powerheads do to plankton?

I would greatly appreciate your thoughts on these matters. Respectfully yours, Charles J. Matthews, M.D., P.A.

A. Leave it to a physician to try and make things more complicated than necessary! Oh, all right you are sincere, and respectful, so I shouldn't pick on you, but hey I can't resist and let's face it: you definitely are taking a simple method and trying to make it complicated.

Last month I discussed some of the issues you bring up, but not all of them. Please review that column. Regarding your heating cable idea, many people have thought about this for a moment at least, considering the parallel concepts of concentration gradient diffusion of water through the substrate in Jaubert's system and convection movement of water through the substrate in freshwater planted tanks, first promoted widely by Dupla in the book *The Optimum Aquarium.* I have never used a heating cable system because I simply do not think it offers an advantage over natural diffusion, considering the added complexity of having this extra device. I can see the potential for a difference in the effect achieved by heating water in the substrate, namely more rapid turnover of water through it, so I am not saying that the heating cables do nothing, they certainly work. Lifting water from a reducing environment up to the oxidizing environment via convection has the potential to supply otherwise inaccessible nutrients to some plants and, in a marine aquarium this should also stimulate growth in algae (including higher seaweeds and undesirable types), but I am speaking from the theoretical position of an arm-chair, not having experimented with the cable systems personally. I think the qualitative changes you saw in your aquarium would have happened anyway, indicative of the maturation of the system biologically, though I don't doubt that the heating cables expedited the situation.

Regarding your second suggestion, I think you may be mis-interpreting the meaning of void space, but it could be that I misunderstood the picture you were describing because you did not describe it well. Void space is the water area separat-ed by a perforated plenum from the overlying gravel. So, did you mean to move the plenum up so that it is in the middle of the sand bed, sandwiched between two sand lay-ers and open to the water in the tank via a pipe? If so, this would work, but for in-tank application I think it is best to have the plenum on the bottom with about four inches of coarse sand over it.

Jaubert anticipated this design as well as vertical systems. If you want to see a further range of ways to employ Jaubert-style filtration you should read the patent referenced at the end of this column.

Regarding your third suggestion, this is yet anther variation of course. Based on what you wrote it seems you don't fully understand what the void space does. The void space actu-ally retains some oxygen and helps to prevent the sand from becoming completely anoxic. In a thick sand layer over a plenum the oxygen level is typically lowest about halfway between the plenum and the upper sand surface in contact with the circulating aquarium water. Many aquarists have the impression that the oxygen level is lowest in the plenum, but that is not the case.

I agree with you that a thick layer of very coarse aragonite sandwiched between two oxygenated layers would work for denitrification, and this is also shown in Jaubert's patent.

On your fourth suggestion you missed a critical point that is one of the most elegant features of the Jaubert system: the organic source of carbon is detritus and dissolved organic material very abundantly available in the substrate of closed system aquariums. There is no shortage of food for the bacteria. I know of no-one who has tried to enhance this natural process by diffusing organic food into the sand. In general it simply is unnecessary since the system works completely well without the added organic carbon. However, systems with a very high fish biomass can exceed the capacity of the sand bed to bring the nitrate to zero. Normally such systems can be filtered better by simply adding more sand (a thicker layer) or additional sand/plenum area in attached reservoirs. Your question brings up the possibility that the limiting factor in high fish load systems is not just surface area but also, possibly, organic food. I suspect that is not the case since the higher biomass should also mean higher organic food availability. Adding organic carbon as methanol or glucose might provide some additional capacity to denitrify the system, but I suspect it also might increase the possibility of encouraging the development of pathogenic bacteria such as strains of *Vibrio* which are normally present in the biological community of the sand bed, but kept in check by other competing organisms. What I mean is that nutrient enrichment might preferentially favor one type of bacteria, altering the natural community population, but I have not tested this. Perhaps you can look into this since you are a physician.

Your fifth question I have answered a few times before. The skimmer does not impede the function of Jaubert's filter since organic carbon is available as particulate detritus trapped in the sand bed. Nevertheless I don't doubt that one could do an experiment and discover that there is enhanced capacity to denitrify when the skimmer is shut off, kind of like nutrient enrichment just described. The skimmer also reduces the quantity of nitrogenous waste available to the bacteria, which is not a disadvantage. It helps reduce the "load" on the filter for systems with a high fish population.

Your sixth question regarded plankton friendliness of pumps. Please review last month's column for details about that. In a nutshell: don't worry about it.

References

Jaubert, J. 1991. United States Patent number 4,995,980.

May 1997

No questions this month. I decided to focus on an important problem affecting reef aquariums AND reefs in the natural environment. In the March column I talked about the coral disease called "RTN," (short for rapid tissue necrosis) and, just in time for me to write about it for this month's column I had an episode of it take place in my 15 gallon reef. I write about it not just to commiserate with fellow reef keeping hobbyists, but to share some fascinating observations about this event in my tank. Before I get to the fascinating part I'm afraid I have to share a somewhat long (and maybe not so fascinating) history of the event.

How it all began: a.ka. too many variables to even guess

I came home from work one day with a few fragments of two of the several *Acropora* species growing in the office aquarium at Two Little Fishies. I had decided to make room for them in my home aquarium since they were species growing only in the office, and I wanted to have them in at least two aquariums to decrease the chance of losing them to disease. The more tanks that one uses for growing cuttings of the same species the less likely that the species will be lost.

In my aquarium at home I cleared out some undergrowth of old dead branches of *Acropora* and glued the two largest fragments in place with AquaStik, as I have done before many times. I also pulled out some irridescent blue *Coelothrix*, a beautiful alga, as well as some zoanthid anemones, all to make room for the largest of the new *Acropora* fragments. The smaller fragments I placed in another aquarium. The zoanthids leaked milky fluid into the water when severed from their attachments.*

*In my experience the "juice" from zoanthids seems to stress corals. It may contain toxins.

While I was at it that night I made further changes to my 15 gallon aquarium that require more preliminary explanation. I had just within a few weeks put a new Eheim hobby pump in the sump, thereby increasing the water flow returning to the reef tank. This new pump is connected to a UPS battery back-up system that keeps it going for eight hours during a power outage. The new pump was so much stronger than the eight year old one in use that I decided to take the eight year old one out of service the night I put the coral fragments in. This gave me even more room for the coral fragments since I removed the zoanthid encrusted water return pipe. In the future I plan to install a smaller capacity pump as a secondary return should the new primary one ever fail, but that is besides the point I intend to make here, which is that I made quite a few changes that night! An additional "change" existed in the system for about two weeks already: the Tunze skimmer in the sump was shut off because the motor brakes had broken (it had worked reliably for five years up to this point).

My story here is starting to sound like one of those long letters I hesitate to answer, so it's time to get to the meaty parts. OK, I checked the corals at midnight just before I went to bed, and everything in the tank was just fine. When I awoke at 7 the following morning the new corals were still just fine, but I could see that all of the *Pocillopora damicornis* colonies were losing tissue and had large areas of exposed white skeleton. This kind of scene can effectively make even the best aquarist feel like sucking his/her thumb!

Here was a disease that nearly wiped out one species in just seven hours, and it was so widespread already that it was impossible to isolate. I did what any other sane aquarists would do confronted with this scene at this time in the morning. I let out a rather audible moan and left the room immediately to get some breakfast. When I came back for another look I found that my nightmare had not vanished: it was quite real.

I siphoned some water from another tank into a 5 gallon bucket and added Neomycin sulfate to this treatment bucket at a dosage of ca. 200mg/gallon. It was the only antibiotic I had available at the time. I proceeded to break off as much as I could of the largest colonies of *Pocillopora* and placed them in the bucket. They had grown from planula larvae and were attached to the glass. The species is a prolific producer of planula larvae (by asexual means) and there are colonies throughout the tank. I could not remove all of this species since it is so widespread and well encrusted in the tank. I figured I should be able to save at least some of it by breaking out the big pieces. I used Lugol's solution (potassium iodide with iodine -an antiseptic) to spot treat encrusting colonies left in the tank. I administered the Lugol's with an eyedropper directly over the colonies. Of course my real worry was that this was just the beginning of an unstoppable fire that would run through all of the corals in the tank--- a real possibility.

By the evening when I returned home I noticed that the disease had not progressed in the *Pocillopora* (neither in the aquarium nor in the bucket), but it had affected the single small colony of *Seriatopora hystrix*, which is in the same family as *Pocillopora damicornis*. I spot treated the *Seriatopora hystrix* with Lugol's iodine.

I was scrutinizing the aquarium especially closely by this time and noticed some peculiar things. First, I noticed that the serpent starfish were not healthy. Some had developed holes in their disc and others had dropped parts of their legs. Second, all colonies of *Pocillopora damicornis* in the 15 gallon tank were affected, from large to small newly settled ones. However, colonies settled in the attached refugium aquarium, which is exposed to the same water, were not affected. By the next day there were already new colonies settling on the glass since the event seemed to trigger release of planula larvae. The colonies in the bucket also released larvae. The larvae were unaffected and settled without incident. It seemed that by the time I intervened the disease had mostly run its course like a fire that burned out quickly. I don't know if my intervention in this case had any positive influence in halting the progress of the disease. The "yellow polyps" (yellow zoanthids) also were affected slightly, evidenced by shortening of the tentacles and poor expansion of the polyps. After a few more days the yellow polyps recovered and there was no further progression of tissue loss in the *Pocillopora* nor in the *Seriatopora*. It was apparent that the "coast was clear" and I returned the broken colonies to the aqarium, gluing them back in place with AquaStik. The tissue was starting to grow back already on all affected colonies.

My experience differs from most in that the disease burned out quickly. In most cases it is not easy to extinguish the progression of the tissue loss, though virulent strains have been stopped effectively and completely with Chloramphenical, based on the advice of Craig Bingman (Bruce Carlson, pers. comm.). The concensus now, however, is that treatment of the display tank with antibiotics is risky since death and decomposition of large populations of bacteria in the live sand and rocks can cause a dramatic oxygen demand on the system leading to suffocation of the animals. The corals are best treated in a separate aquarium.

Regarding the serpent stars, I am reminded of a question I received about serpent stars falling apart after being introduced into an aquarium. The question appeared in my June 1996 column. One possibility that I did not explore in my answer in that column was a virulent type of pathogenic bacteria. I now strongly suspect this could have been be the culprit. Also affected in the aquarium from the June 1996 column were sea cucumbers. As a side note, I have seen sea cucumbers succumb (that sounds interesting, doesn't it? say it three times fast) to a sudden condition that causes tissue necrosis and immobility and then death within a day. It usually strikes holding tanks in which a large number of sea cucumbers are being kept prior to shipping. A similar phenomenon can be seen with *Astraea* snails being held in large numbers in the same aquarium.

I am reminded of Martin Moe's assertion, "Now that serious marine aquarists have a better understanding of what is required..., and access to the equipment that can provide good marine environments for many invertebrates, a lot of the more mysterious problems that we encounter are probably caused by bacteria." This statement preceeds a series of fascinating accounts that Martin noticed "popped out at (him) over the years," all cleverly juxtaposed in his revised edition of *The Marine Aquarium Handbook* (Moe, 1992). The accounts relate his own experience and that of other aquaculturists and aquarium hobbyists in the management, with antibiotic treatments, of mysterious rapid mortalities in fishes and invertebrates, some caused by bacteria in the genus *Vibrio*. This section is one of many gems in this book. If Martin makes any further revisions to it I think he should include the experience of RTN as another example of bacteria causing devastatingly rapid mortality.

An article by Mike Paletta in the Fall 1996 issue of *SeaScope* discusses the occurence of "bleaching" in small-polyped stony corals and proposes a pathogen, *Vibrio* spp. bacteria. Lo and behold the same bad guys Moe discussed. Paletta's article was particularly interesting to me because it highlights an important error of detail that exists in both the scientific and aquarium hobbyist communities. This error surrounds the use of the term "bleaching." It is unfortunate that this word was chosen since it does not precisely convey the meaning of the several maladies that affect corals, causing them to become pale. What is causing the whitening? Are the corals losing tissue or just pigment? The question of the difference between the two options can be more basically asked: are the corals dead or just faded? Quite a difference! In large polyp fleshy corals there is no confusion since the tissue is very obvious. In the small polyped corals there is considerable confusion since the tissue is rather thinly covering the skeleton. Paletta's article, while it focuses on a rather important topic and offers new information, fails to adequately distinguish in its title what is happening in these so-called "bleaching" events: the corals are dying fast from tissue destruction, not from losing pigment. The title should not have been "Bleaching of Small Polyp Stony Corals in Aquaria." It should have been "Rapid tissue loss and death in Small-Polyped Stony Corals in Aquaria."

In general, scientific articles describing "bleaching" refer to the loss of pigment, not tissue. This malady is quite different from RTN, is seldom fatal, and has numerous causes. However, it is likely that even scientists could make the same error in judgement that aquarists make about small polyped stony corals, especially when compiling statistics about "coral bleaching," based on the observations of other people around the world. When divers report bleaching events do they really know how to distinguish loss of pigment from loss of tissue?

During the RTN event in my tank I had a close look at the bottom of my sump, which had developed a fairly thick layer of settled out detritus. Close inspection revealed some blackened areas of hydrogen sulfide in the detritus, which I carefully sucked out with a turkey baster. The cessation of operation of the protein skimmer located in this sump caused a reduction of dissolved oxygen and water motion there. Since the skimmer was off, an increase in dissolved organic compound availability, which increases biological oxygen demand, may have promoted the development of anoxic conditions in the detritus that had accumulated in the sump. Could such anoxic sites promote the development of pathogenic strains of bacteria? I can't say for sure but I believe there could be a connection.

Elevated temperature (associated with both bleaching and tissue loss events in the wild) reduces oxygen solubility in the water and therefore increases the possibility of anoxic conditions in the substrate. In nature the warm season is usually also the calm season, which further increases the chance of anoxia in the substrate in the natural environment, or brings the anoxic condition closer to the substrate surface. If an anoxic environment is a breeding ground for pathogenic bacteria, then hot and calm water are dangerous conditions for corals sensitive to bacterial diseases. Coincidentally (?) coral diseases in the natural environment seem to be most prevalent in the warmer months.

Lately there has been a lot of publicity in the news about tissue necrosis diseases in corals, including the long recognized "white band" disease and more recently dicovered similar conditions such as "white pox" described by Dr. Jim Porter based on affected colonies of *Acropora palmata* off Key West. The news media has reported these conditions, usually associated with the need for conservation and protection from human influences (which probably have absolutely nothing to do with these diseases). At the same time avid aquarists have been writing their experience and hypotheses in E-mail communications. Terry Siegel, Stanley Brown, Bruce Carlson, Craig Bingman, Bob Stark, Charles Delbeek, Larry Jackson, Greg Schiemer, and Greg Cook among others have offered interesting perspectives and described their personal experiences, losses and successes that have shaped my views about this condition. The combined pool of experience of these people and all of you aquarists is an invaluable resource for scientists studying these diseases. At the moment scientists haven't got a clue about the causes of tissue necrosis diseases, if the newspaper articles are reporting their opinions accurately.

References

Moe, M. A. Jr. (1992) *The Marine Aquarium Handbook 2nd Edition Revised.* Green Turtle Publications. 318 Pp.

Paletta, M. (1996) Bleaching of Small Polyp Stony Corals in Aquaria. *SeaScope*. Fall 1996.

June 1997

How does your algae grow?

Many aquarists using a kalkreactor for the first time have reported an increase in the growth of filamentous algae. This is to be expected since CO_2 is a fertilizer for the plants. Furthermore, while the use of kalkwasser keeps dissolved phosphate in the aquarium low by causing a precipitation of phosphate and enhancing phosphate export via the protein skimmer, the use of a kalkreactor does not offer these benefits, so dissolved phosphate tends to be higher in systems using the kalkreactor exclusively. This accumulation of phosphate can be managed through extra protein skimming, and the harvesting of higher algae. There has been some speculation among aquarists that older systems especially, which relied for years on kalkwasser additions to assist dissolved phosphate control, might see a sudden increase in dissolved phosphate (and increase in algae growth) when switching to the kalkreactor system. The reasoning was that the extra CO_2 in the water and resulting suppression of pH would tend to dissolve phosphate precipitated on the gravel. Although it seems intuitive that it might, CO_2 does not cause precipitated phosphate to dissolve. Nor does a slight decrease in pH cause a release of phosphate from the gravel or other substrates. However, it is common experience to see an increase in phosphate in the water plus a dramatic and sometimes difficult to control growth of algae when switching to the kalkreactor system. This increase in algal growth is due mainly to the availability of CO_2 during the light period (thus enhancing photosynthesis) and also to the decrease in phosphate EXPORT when a kalkreactor is used instead of kalkwasser.*

*It is also true that if the calcareous substrate being dissolved in the reactor contains a significant amount of phosphate, the effluent from the reactor will contain some of this dissolved phosphate. This phosphate will spontaneously precipitate at the high pH of the aquarium, but it may contribute to increased algae growth. Manufacturers of calcium reactors now sell calcareous substrates with very low phosphate content.

Speculation that the increased algae growth seen is caused by liberation of old reserves of precipitated phosphate is therefore incorrect. Well, actually there is an indirect truth to it. Algae are able to uptake inorganic phosphorus and organic nitrogen from the substrate through their stolons or root-like growths. Endocellular bacteria living in the algal tissues assist in this process. If there is more phosphate precipitated in the substrate, it stands to reason that the "fuel reserves" for such algae are greater. Stimulation of the algae by the availability of CO_2 during the photoperiod promotes algae to grow, and they may be further "fed" by the available phosphate in the water if that is not limited sufficiently by protein skimming or kalkwasser additions. Even if the dissolved phosphate is kept very low, the precipitated phosphate is still available to algae growing on the rocks, sand, or gravel. So giving them a little fertilizer, such as CO_2 or iron for instance, can give them the opportunity to grow explosively. It doesn't take much to make the algae grow. That is why herbivores are so important to keep the growth in check. For further information about how algae are able to uptake inorganic phosphorous and organic nitrogen from the substrate please refer to *Nature International Weekly Journal of Science*, volume 381 No. 6581 May 30, 1996. In it there is a scientific correspondence titled "Roots in mixotrophic algae" from professor J. Jaubert, J. R. M. Chisholm, C. Dauga, E. Ageron, and P. A. D. Grimont.

Q. Dear Julian,
I'm starting to set up a 55 gallon reef tank. The dimensions of the tank are 48"L x 20"H x 13"W. To keep the cost down I have decided to set up my system based on an article I read in FAMA. The system was called the Handy Reef by Tom Miller which is based on Dr. Jean Jaubert's system with the exception of adding a skimmer. I'm following this set up exactly as Tom Miller did except that I'm using a Berlin Skimmer rather than a Skilter. The skimmer will sit behind the tank with the pump inside, located at the surface of the water. Will this be sufficient this way?

My lighting consists of four 48" bulbs, two "03" and two Vitalite. The lights will be staggered. I chose the Vitalites due to their high CRI. I have a reflector in the hood with a fan to help reduce the heat. The "03" and the Vitalites will be on two different timers. Due to the depth of the plenum and substrate, five and one half inches total, I will lose one quarter of my depth. Will the lighting be sufficient to sustain and grow anemones and corals?

I will use live sand, Tom Miller recommends 12 lbs for a 55 gallon tank. This is supposed to reduce the amount of live rock I will need since you are supposed to leave most of the sand uncovered. What he did not say is how much live rock you should use. What I would like to know is approximately how much live rock to use. What is the minimum amount and how high to stack the rock?

For tank circulation I only have one powerhead at this time. It is a Rio 200. I know this is small, but I wanted to put it lower in the tank for slower movement. What I need to know is how strong of a pump to use at the surface. Would it be better to use them both at the surface, or was this a good idea? I'm also relying on my return from my skimmer to help with circulation. I have an Emperor 400 from a fish only tank that I would like to use. I know you say that you don't need any biological filtration other than the rock and sand, but it allows for good water movement and has a good place for mechanical filtration. What do you think?

The fish I would like to have are as follows: Two clowns with their anemone, three green chromis, one royal gramma, one yellow tang. Can you recommend some good cleaner fish, crabs, or shrimp to add? I would also like a star fish. Can you recommend one? Can I put coral in with an anemone?

John Drabek
Oklahoma City, OK

A. Dear John,
Yes your system will work. The lighting is sufficient, and so is the skimming. However, there are some points I'd like to clarify because they affect your potential for complete success.

When you mentioned 12 pounds of live sand for a 55 gallon tank I presume you meant as a seed stock to get the culture going in the rest of the sand, which you probably are buying dry from a local dealer. The approximately four and a half inches of sand depth you are planning will certainly weigh more than 12 pounds! Many readers will be astonished at the depth you plan, but in fact it is the correct depth for a Jaubert type system. The plenum has about one inch in height giving you a total of about five and a half inches height from the bottom of the tank to the top of the sand. I have set up and maintained about a dozen Jaubert systems now and I have played around with different sand bed depths and different coarseness of sand. I have also had the opportunity to visit with Jaubert and see his systems. Something I want to emphasize is that if you use too fine a sand the diffusion through the bed is so impeded that the system does not function properly. So the "sand" must be coarse. The oatmeal size pieces of broken shell, coral, and *Halimeda* of the readily available Carib Sea's Geo-Marine Aragonite provide a properly sized substrate to work with.

I have seen discussion about using different size media in different layers to create different zones in the sand bed. This is completely unnecessary and the concept probably originates from a misunderstanding of the natural zonation which becomes established within the sand bed despite it being of uniform composition. Perhaps this hybrid idea of using different grades of sand in layers as promoted by some aquarists is an artifact of the concept of mechanical filtration with sand, where the layers provide a means of sorting out finer particulate matter. A Jaubert system is not a mechanical filter, however. It works by diffusion and the best way to encourage this diffusion is to use a coarse material.

*Um, not always. It may have a high nitrate (NO_3) level, but often it does not. It is more likely for the plenum water to have a high nitrite (NO_2) level because the oxygen level there is low.

Fine sand in a thin layer (1/2 inch or so) may be used for aesthetics on a tank bottom without a plenum, but it does not have the capacity to bring the nitrate down as low as a Jaubert system using a plenum and coarse sand (which can be incorporated within the tank or in an attached refugium-see *Reef Notes* Vol. One). The height of the sand over the plenum in a Jaubert system allows the formation of distinct oxygen level zones in the sand and isolation of the plenum water from the main body of water in the aquarium. If the sand bed is not thick enough, the zones are not established and the plenum water, which has a high nitrate level*, may seep up into the main body of water.

Setting up such a system is simple. After you put saltwater in the aquarium, put the plenum in place and shake out any trapped air bubbles. Then put the gravel on top of it to hold the plenum in place. After you have put about two inches of gravel over the plenum, put a layer of screen down to prevent burrowing organisms from digging too deeply. Then top it off with another (approximately) two and a half inches. A variation to this method has been developed by the company Reef Renovators. They use a thick black plastic mesh over the plenum (black DLS material for you old timers) to prevent burrowers from disturbing the lower sand/gravel layer just above the plenum. This is a very effective design.

With such a thick sand/gravel layer over a plenum you don't need to have any rock at all to set up a successful reef aquarium. You could literally glue live corals to the walls of the aquarium with underwater epoxy and just let them grow into a reef structure. However, live rock is interesting to look at too and it does bring additional diversity of life into the tank. So, to answer your question, there is no specific amount of live rock required. You can put in as much or as little as you wish to achieve the aesthetic "look" you desire. One work of caution regarding a subject you briefly touched upon. You don't want to have the rock covering too much of the bottom. It is true that much of the sand should be "uncovered" as you said. This allows for proper diffusion of dissolved gasses and nitrogenous waste to take place through the bed. In addition, the larger the quantity of coralline coated rock you have exposed to the light the larger the demand on the calcium from the water. So, less rock in general means less calcium consumption. Of course if you don't use rock but instead glue stony corals all over the glass you will very quickly develop a high calcium demand too.

Why not consider soft corals, zoanthids, and corallimorpharian "mushroom anemones?" Most will do very well in the system you have planned. In my experience *Xenia* species do very well in Jaubert type systems (keep the anemone away, however, as it will injure them). Leather corals such as Sarcophyton, *Lobophytum*, and *Sinularia* species are hardy and compatible with anemones, though the soft corals' points of contact with an anemone will usually remain "bald" (closed polyps). Zoanthids will also close up where the anemone contacts them, but otherwise are quite suitable additions for this tank. Several colonies of the "button polyps" *Protopalythoa* spp. in brown with green centers, "Yellow Polyps," or the multi-colored *Zoanthus* spp. would make for interesting patterns of color. You have ideal lighting for showing off and growing the many hued "mushroom" or disc anemones. You could build fields of different varieties in red, blue, and green since they are all compatible with each other. Leave room between corallimorphs and zoanthids since the corallimorphs usually will injure zoanthids.

Regarding the anemone, for such a tank I recommend that you choose one of the following: *Stichodactyla haddoni* (the "Saddle Anemone"), or *Macrodactyla doreensis* (the "Corkscrew" or "Long Tentacle" Anemone). These are hardy anemones that will likely thrive in your aquarium. Also, they will bury their column in the sand next to a rock and will tend to stay in that spot. Other clownfish host anemones are more likely to wander and are not as hardy.

Regarding your fish, that sounds like a nice population, though the Green Chromis would probably be better as a larger school, such as five instead of three. You have to be careful about the fish getting caught in the anemone! This is really quite a small tank you are planning, worsened by the fact the width is only 13 inches. I don't like such tall narrow tanks. If you can make the change now, use a wider tank such as a 75 gallon, which is 18 inches wide. The anemone will plant itself on the bottom, so building a reef structure up to some height away from the anemone will give the fish a safe refuge.

One very important note: Sand beds consume a lot of oxygen! I'm not certain that your water movement plans will provide sufficient aeration at night for the fishes. I have seen fish die at night from low oxygen levels in aquaria with sand beds. Simply using an airstone or two (with a good supply of air) in the tank to lift the bottom water to the top will work. Using sufficient quantity of power heads to achieve the same purpose will also work. I make a point of this here because in my experience if you are planning a large population of fish, you need really strong circulation to maintain adequate oxygen levels at night. Fine air bubbles unfortunately lead to salt creep buildup around the tank.

One last note. In a "handy reef" if the tank has no surface skimming overflow and therefore no plumbing, while it is easy to set up, you may notice a surface film develops. This film impedes light penetration and gas exchange. Having a surface skimming overflow that drains into a sump from which water is pumped back into the tank provides two important benefits: 1.) the surface film is skimmed off and mixed into the water where it can be broken down or removed by the protein skimmer; and 2.) the skimming off of the surface water causes bottom water to rise and helps maintain oxygen levels at night, a very important consideration that I just emphasized.

You asked about crabs I might recommend. Well, if you get a *Stichodactyla haddoni*, you can try a small porcelain crab which lives on the anemone. It is a filter feeder, and its association with the anemone is nice to watch. Star fish, a.k.a. "seastars" are generally best avoided. The blue seastar, *Linckia laevigata* is reasonably hardy and long lived, if you find a healthy one. Serpent stars are very nice additions to such an aquarium, however, and you could easily house about ten of them in this tank. They make a fascinating wriggly sight at feeding time! For shrimp you might try *Lysmata amboinensis*, the scarlet cleaner. It will pick parasites from the fish. I don't recommend cleaner wrasses, but i you want a cleaner fish you might try a pair of neon gobies, available now as tank-raised specimens.

December 1997   The Saga of "Big Guy"

Once in a while something like this happens that just makes for a story that's got to be told. While I was in the home stretch finishing up the text, captions, and helping with photograph color corrections for *The Reef Aquarium* Volume Two I got a phone call from my friend Chris Fonzi. He was desperate, though his typical calm attitude did not relay that fact. That he needed to call about this problem meant something was seriously up. There was something wrong with Big Guy. Big Guy is an approximately 5 year old "Wolf-eel Blenny," *Congrogadus subduscens*. The common name for this type of fish is a mis-identification. It is not really a blenny nor an eel nor a wolf eel. In fact it is most closely related to members of the genus *Pseudochromis*, the little brightly colored basslets. This species grows quite large and is a pretty voracious fish eater that has a whole lot of charm if you don't mind its dietary requirement of the occasional live fish.

Big Guy is quite an intelligent fish, as anyone who sees it can attest. About two years ago at a Christmas party Chris and his fiancee Gina told me they were concerned about Big Guy because he had a strange habit of biting his own tail, often to the point of bleeding. I was both amused and intrigued by this abnormal behaviour, offering the opinion that Big guy must be bored, and that he needed company. Fish psychology must be considered, in addition to the usual matters of water quality and such.

Well, Chris and Gina put some other fish in there with Big Guy and he did eventually come around and started becoming more social. What prompted Chris to call me about Big Guy this time was that he started biting his tail again, to the point that he developed a serious infection. You might wonder why the habit returned. The cause was simple. Chris and Gina had just moved to a new home. It seems that the move upset Big Guy and he developed a serious case of anxiety.

Chris told me that the wound was pretty yucky, red and white with loose flesh, and that Big Guy was breathing fast, with exaggerated gill movement. He was also listless. Based on what Chris described, it sounded like Big Guy had not only an external infection at the site of the wound, but also a systemic infection. I explained to Chris that Big Guy was on his last leg, er, fin and probably was history, but there was a chance to save him if the right antibiotic was administered. The trouble is, I explained, you generally can't get effective treatments at your pet store. I told him that he might be able to get nitrofurazone at a pet store, though it was unlikely to save the fish since the condition was so advanced. "What the fish needs, Chris, is an injectable antibiotic," I told him. Chris said he wanted to try the nitro-furazone. I told him to treat Big Guy in a hospital tank, not

to treat the main display, but to do a water change on the
display anyway. So Chris called me back after several days
to give me a report. He had treated the display tank with
nitrofurazone, completely against my advice. And he also
did several water changes. Big Guy did not get better. But
he did not get much worse. I told him he was lucky and that
Big Guy definitely had a chance to survive, because he
would have been dead by now otherwise. In the meantime
I had contacted Dr. John Gratzek at the University of
Georgia to discuss the case. I know Dr. Gratzek from the
Fish Health Management Course he organizes every August
(see last month's column for info about the course). He told
me that Eric Johnson, a Fish Vet, lives in Atlanta and would
likely be able to help Chris. I had also met Eric at the Fish
Health Management Short Course a few years back, and
now it seemed we had a plan because Eric knew how to
inject fish. I did a little more research to figure out what drug
to use. I consulted with Dr. Gratzek and Dr. D. Aron, also
from the University of Georgia. We talked about what antibiotics to use and where to inject: dorsal musculature (back
muscles) vs. intraperitoneal "I.P." (in the belly). I also called
Dr. Mike Bodri, who I had met at a veterinary conference
where he had invited me to be a guest speaker. I knew Dr.
Bodri had considerable experience and interest in the use of
antibiotics to treat aquatic organisms. He suggested we try a
drug called Baytril and to do an I.P. injection. So this is what
I told Chris to do. And he contacted Eric Johnson to perform
the procedure. It was enormously convenient that Chris
lives only about a half hour from Eric Johnson.

Success!
I don't know whether it was the medication, all the fuss and
attention, or both, but Big Guy made a stunning recovery,
which was certainly gratifying for all parties concerned. I
received the following E-mail message from Chris:

"Yes, Big Guy is well on the road to recovery and sends his
thanks. Next time you're here, I'm sure he'll want to give
you a big, wet kiss. The second shot went well enough.
Since he is a Fonzi, we figured that finding his butt would
be easy, but it was more challenging than we anticipated.
Also, the boy was beginning to associate leaving his cave

with pain and was in danger of becoming a recluse for awhile there. On top of that, he is getting to the age when he will realize he is different from the other kids and we, like any parents, are concerned about his long-term development and scholarship potential. Unless his intellectual development picks up, I'm afraid he will do no better than the University of Georgia.

Gina and "Big Guy"
Photo by Chris Fonzi.

Sad news- Big Guy passed away this year, after he developed what appeared to be tumors in his eyes.

His tail looks like it's beginning to heal and his appetite has returned. He finally ate the Lazarous goldfish. Also, he has taken up his old hobbies, including lengthy discussions with Gina and moving pieces of rock around with his mouth. Like most men, he only does the moving... Gina tells him where the pieces should go.

Thanks again for all your help. I'll send you a picture shortly to enhance your emotional involvement."

And so, with a happy ending I give you the image of Gina and Big Guy, who obviously have a special relationship!

Q. I just can't seem to keep angelfish. My first one, a *C. flavicauda*, died after 5 years in my tank. That death occurred after the GFI on the tank had tripped and the power was out for about 18 hours. I attributed his death to low oxygen levels.

Today I lost his successor, a cherub (don't recall, maybe *C. argi?*) angel, after only 2 1/2 years. Two days ago he was fine. I came home yesterday and he was lying on the bottom breathing hard, and occasionally getting up and swimming around. All other fish in the tank, including two tangs, were fine. It was a hot day, and that tank has no skimmer, so I thought his problem might again be caused by lack of oxygen. I took the skimmer air pump from the other tank (the biggest air pump I have) and put some airstones in the tank, then went back to work. That evening, he was up and swimming around normally. However, I was still worried, because he did not show any interest in food (very unusual for him). Today, I went home in the afternoon, and he was again lying on the bottom breathing hard, and not getting up. His fins looked a little raggy, although all of the other fish were ignoring him. I decided that it was too late to do anything, and took him out to euthanize him, but he died in a little bucket of water soon after I took him out of the tank.

I saved the body in the freezer. My question is, how can I determine the cause of death? I've never done an autopsy, and somehow it seems a lot more difficult to dissect an animal that used to eat from your fingers than one that came from a bucket of formaldehyde in Biology class. I don't know much about fish pathology (or anatomy, for that matter) I just want to know why I can't seem to keep angels on a long-term basis. It's true his diet has been pretty poor in the last month, mostly Spirulina flakes, brine shrimp, and occasional scallops or frozen food, but one month of poor diet shouldn't cause death (my diet has been pretty bad too, ten days and counting until I defend for my Ph.D.).

Teresa

A. Dear Teresa (Dr. Teresa I hear now, congratulations!) I have experienced the situation you describe a few times with various fish, including angelfish. I suspect the culprit is hydrogen sulfide, to which they are apparently very sensitive. I wrote to you via E-mail and according to my advice you checked for but did not find any telltale black areas in the gravel. Nevertheless the symptoms you describe and the circumstance lead me to believe that there was hydrogen sulfide building up somewhere in the system whether in the bottom substrate or in a rock, and that it periodically burped out to the demise of your angelfish. I talked about this a little bit last month in reference to the "mysterious death of the last fish added" syndrome. Please refer to that column.

Problems with hydrogen sulfide are most prevalent in systems with a thick bottom substrate and/or a bottom substrate that is especially fine. Having a lot of live rock in a thick stack over the thick bottom substrate virtually guarantees hydrogen sulfide containing pockets will form. The development of hydrogen sulfide occurs in pockets where oxygen is depleted, especially in the presence of organic material (i.e. detritus or a dead thing). Preventing the occurrence of hydrogen sulfide is not always possible, but the risk of its formation can be reduced by having a loose rock construction and employing very strong water motion. Bottom sifters also help to prevent dead pockets from developing in the bottom substrate. When there is not enough water circulation the oxygen level in the water falls, as you noted. This is particularly problematic at night when the plants are not producing oxygen but consuming it instead. Power outages can be brutal too, so investing in a battery backup system (UPS) to run a circulating pump is a good idea.

I had to laugh reading your letter, because instead of asking about the mysterious sudden illness and death of your fish, you suggested that you were somehow unsuccessful maintaining angelfish. While they certainly can live much longer than five years, that length of time in captivity is not an indication of failure! By the way, you mentioned doing an autopsy on the fish. Well, you really meant a necropsy of course. An autopsy is a examination of a dead human by another human. One thing to check with these fish is the gills. The symptom of rapid gilling and lethargy can also be attributed to protozoan parasites. However, I think that it is unlikely that your fish were infested with parasites considering your experience level and the fishes' time in captivity. However, it would be a good idea to check the gills just to rule out parasitic infestation. The ragged appearance you mentioned does suggest the possibility of bacterial infection. It is possible the fish succumbed to attack by a Vibrio sp. bacterium, as these are indicated in rapid mortalities like you described.

Q. Dear Julian

I read your column several months ago regarding Calcium reactors and the inherent problems with aragonite media (coral gravel such as Carib Sea) that was being used. You noted that when dissolved in the low pH environment of the reactor, such media can release phosphate into the water. I was wondering, in light of the German imported media (Coralith, Super Kalk Gold, and others) that have come into the US, have you reconsidered your position about these reactors? These media have been shown to contain virtually no phosphates, and tanks running reactors with these media have not exhibited the (algae) problems associated with (dissolving natural) aragonite.

Sincerely, Perry Tishgart, Wyndmoor, PA

A. Dear Perry,

It turns out a lot of people were put off by my comments about calcium reactors. Many people use them quite successfully and these aquarists and the manufacturers wondered about what I meant to say. Actually, I don't mean to criticise calcium reactors and did not intend to do so in the column. They are a viable and technically simple means of maintaining calcium and alkalinity levels to support the growth of rapidly calcifying corals. What I was pointing out, as you noted, was the sometimes noted problem with stimulation of algae growth when a calcium reactor is added to an established system. The cause of this problem is twofold. One being the use of media that release phosphate upon being dissolved by the CO_2. You addressed that issue, and in fact the use of calcium carbonate media that are virtually phosphate free does make a big difference in preventing the stimulation of algal growth. So, I agree with you that the reactors should be run with such media. The second cause for algal growth is the CO_2 itself, of course, as I mentioned in that previous article. The availability of CO_2 during the light period can enhance the growth of algae. However, it also may enhance the growth of coralline algae that by their coating growths prevent the establishment of undesirable filamentous species. The presence of herbivores is also really a critical factor in keeping algae growth in check. The use of protein skimming, in addition, ensures a means of phosphate export for systems using a calcium reactor, and helps to blow off excess CO_2 (maintaining equilibrium with the atmospheric concentration).

I hesitate to say more about calcium reactors since my experience with them is limited to the comments I've received from people using them. Most of the comments have been positive, which is encouraging. I am setting up a calcium reactor on one of my aquariums so that I can write from personal experience rather than from the armchair. I'll report my experience here in Reef Notes of course.

Magnificent Mangroves

Freshwater and Marine aquarists alike are experiencing renewed interest in planted, natural aquariums, and I believe we will soon come to appreciate a tree, the Red Mangrove, *Rhizophora mangle*, that is suitable to grow in both fresh and salt water. Considering the beauty and ease of care of these trees, they should become very popular. With this article I intend to provide a little natural history information about mangroves, and stimulate interest in them as an ornamental plant for marine and freshwater aquariums or even ponds, provided the temperature is not allowed to approach freezing for extended periods. I should caution the reader that harming or removing mangrove trees is illegal, so I am not proposing that you go out and get a tree. The seeds of mangroves are plentiful, and it is legal to gather them.

Mangroves are distinguished by the ability to thrive in salty soil or in the sea. This ability to adapt is managed by at least three regulatory processes: secretion, exclusion, and accumulation, plus the ability to retain water. Mangrove leaves also have a shiny surface. This cuticle is an adaptation to prevent water loss. Minute glands in the surface of the leaves on some mangroves allow secretion of excess salt, and rain washes the secreted salt away. Some mangroves exclude the salt from entering their roots by means of tissues that allow water passage but not salt...a natural R.O. filter! Some species of mangrove can also accumulate salt in older leaves that soon fall away with their load.

Mangroves typically grow in waterlogged, anaerobic soil, mud, or sand. They may also take root in limestone rock or on top of coral heads. Their roots in anaerobic soils do not extend very deep, but spread out laterally instead to provide a secure footing in the loose substrate. These cable roots may produce special breathing structures called pneumatophores that take in oxygen. The Red Mangrove is distinguished by aerial "prop roots" that extend from its branches, trunk, and other aerial roots. These give the impression that the tree could get up and walk like a spider. Aerial roots also take in oxygen, and they provide firm anchoring where they contact the substrate

The seeds of mangroves usually develop into young seedlings called propagules that germinate while still attached to the tree. These propagules are specially adapted for dispersal by water. They come in a variety of shapes and sizes, some like long rods, some like balls, and others like cigars or beans. They are buoyant and can drift for months before taking root in a suitable substrate. Many are lost by washing up high on a sandy beach and drying out in the sun. Long, cigar shaped propagules such as those of our subject, *Rhizophora mangle*, float upright in the water, roots trailing below and leaves sprouting above.

About the only limitation to keeping mangroves in aquariums is their need for enough room to grow upward. This means that a closed canopy should be avoided, generally. I have seen aquariums with canopies and mangroves where the trees were allowed to grow out the back, receiving light from a nearby window. One might reasonably ask how, even with an open aquarium , the mangrove can be prevented from growing too tall. If one prunes the mangrove in the manner recommended for Bonsai tree cultivation, the leaves do become smaller, new branches develop, and a minature tree can be created. In a tall aquarium with a lid it is possible to house such miniaturized trees, and in an open aquarium such pruning prevents the trees from growing too close to the light source.

When I tell other aquarists that mangroves grow perfectly well in freshwater they typically respond with amazement and disbelief that they thought mangroves required saltwater to grow. It would seem that the red mangrove might require some salt as it is not found too far from salt water in its natural habitat. Nevertheless, I have found some growing naturally in freshwater in canals and rivers that lead to saltwater bays. In the southern part of the Florida Everglades and along the gulf coast of Florida they grow in freshwater, but there is a limit to how far they naturally occur from the sea, and I'm not really sure why. Perhaps it is intolerance to drying out, cooler winter temperature further inland, or simply the direction of water flow from land to sea. In aquariums the limiting factor doesn't exist; they can be grown perfectly well in pure freshwater, even soft water. They are quite hardy and adaptable!

I collect red mangrove propagules and grow them in tap water. I found by accident that I could make beautiful clusters of young trees by crowding them together in a plastic container kept filled with tap water and fertilized occasionally with FloraSan. In a couple of months the proliferating roots become so entangled that the trees can hardly be separated. The roots conform to the shape of the container, and when the mass is pulled from the container it has a neat flat root base to sit on...perfect for shallow Bonsai pots if you can keep the peat or other substrate wet at all times. These groupings of trees are also quite aesthetically pleasing inside a freshwater tank, but one must weigh them down by tying a rock to them for ballast; otherwise they float.

In a marine tank these trees can be used to create a whole aquascape or just an accent. In my reef aquarium I plant mangroves on the upper rocks, holding them there with plastic toothpicks untill the roots grow into the rocks and anchor the trees in place. I do have to trim both branches and roots as they grow too large. Corals and anemones soon grow onto the stalk of the tree, a stunning effect when viewed from above. One can tie zoanthid anemones to the stalk with monofilament (fishing) line or sewing thread to speed up this process.

The care of mangroves is simple. One must provide a source of light sufficient to meet their needs and a humid environment. A single fluorescent lamp can be sufficient if it is close enough to the leaves, but it is best to have two or more tubes when using fluorescent light. A pendant metal halide lamp works well for growing them. Light from a window is also sufficient, and it is possible to set up a small aquarium in your window with mangroves...kind of different from the typical potted houseplants. I found that in really dry climate, or in winter when the air indoors tends to by drier, the mangroves seem to require daily misting to keep the leaves from drying up. Under most circumstances, however, misting is not required more than occasionally to wash off salt or dust. Once per week or two is generally sufficient.

Temperature is another important factor in aquariums and in nature. Mangroves thrive in the tropics, though some species extend into temperate regions. Generally they do not tolerate freezing temperatures. In north Florida along the gulf coast whole islands of Red mangrove forest were wiped out by a severe cold front nearly ten years ago. The more tolerant Black mangrove, *Avicennia*, was not affected. Sporadic survivors and new recruits have since filled in the gaps, but for years the islands looked like a pile of bones as the dead mangrove trees bleached in the sun and the guano from seabirds coated them white. If you plan to grow mangroves in a pond or outdoor aquarium, they must not be exposed to cold weather. They do tolerate very warm weather (and water) however, so summertime outdoors presents no problem aside from the need to keep up with evaporation that could leave the trees parched.

I have encountered two problems with growing Red mangroves that are frustrating but manageable: shock and bugs. Mangroves can suffer "shock" when they are moved. This is manifest by wilting leaves or loss of leaves. When the leaves wilt or drop off in a moved plant, I place it in tap water and give it strong illumination. Usually the tree recovers within a few days. If the leaves have all dropped off, the top bud will usually open within 10 days if the tree is placed in tap water and given strong illumination. The second problem I have encountered with mangroves as well as any other aquatic plant that grows leaves out of the water is insects. Mealy bugs, scales and mites are damaging pests that can be difficult to control, particularly when you can't use pesticides because the plants are housed in a fish tank! Fortunately, there are predatory insects that prey upon and control these pests, and they are obtainable from organic gardening suppliers. Mangrove seeds are generally insect free, but houseplants may not be, and fruits (particularly bananas) often bring mealy bugs into the home.

Brackish aquariums can also house mangroves. It is possible to create the natural habitat of the amusing mudskipper fish by incorporating mangroves, sand, and a shallow water level. I remember as a child reading about these frog-like fish in a *National Geographic* magazine that had a photo on the front featuring one out of water adhering to a mangrove. I have seen these biotopes created in numerous public aquariums, sometimes with fake mangroves, but more recently I have seen exhibits done with the real trees and mudskippers. One exhibit I saw at Hagenbecks Tierpark in Hamburg Germany also housed the four-eyed livebearing fish *Anableps anableps*, and since the water level was shallow, they could be viewed from the front, below the water level and above it. This exhibit also featured a tidal change, evidenced by water marks on the glass. With tidal change it would be possible to house some of the nerite and littorinid snails that graze algae off the Mangrove's roots, and possibly Sesarma crabs, or *Uca* species a.k.a. "Fiddler crabs." Another brackish water fish that occurs with mangroves is *Toxotes jaculatrix*, the Archerfish, famed for its spitting ability. With these three very strange fish and the unique mangrove tree one can make a rather special aquarium in brackish water. Other public displays I have seen that feature mangroves include Biosphere 2 in Oracle, AZ, the Löbbecke Museum in Dusseldorf Germany, and the Waikiki Aquarium in Honolulu. New displays of mangroves are also at the Florida Aquarium in Tampa, Florida and the Museum of Science and Discovery in Ft. Lauderdale. The Aquarium in the Oceanographic Museum in Monaco has a display of Japanese mangroves behind the scenes, and may soon develop a public exhibit for them.

Suggested Readings
Crisp, P., Daniel, L., and P. Tortell. *Mangroves In New Zealand. Trees In The Tide*. G.P. Books. 1990.

Odum, W.E. aand Heald, E.J. Trophic analyses of an estuarin mangrove community. *Bull. Mar. Sci.*, Vol. 22, No. 3, 1972, 671-738.

Snedaker, S.C. Mangroves: Their value and perpetuation. *Nature and Resources*, Vol. 14, No. 3, 1978, 6-13.

Teas, H.J. (ed.) *Biology and Ecology of Mangroves*. The Hague, Dr. W. Junk Publishers, 1983.

Tomlinson, P.B. *The Botany of Mangroves*. Cambridge University Press, 1986.